A NOTE ON THE AUTHOR

LILIAN PIZZICHINI has worked for the *Literary Review*, the *Times Literary Supplement* and as writer-in-residence at a prison. Her first book, *Dead Men's Wages: The Secrets of a London Conman and His Family*, won the 2002 Crime Writers' Association Gold Dagger for Non-fiction. Her second, *The Blue Hour: A Portrait of Jean Rhys,* was published in 2009 to critical acclaim. Lilian Pizzichini lives in London.

Lilian Pizzichini

MUSIC NIGHT at the APOLLO

A Memoir of Drifting

BLOOMSBURY

LONDON · NEW DELHI · NEW YORK · SYDNEY

Bloomsbury Paperbacks
An imprint of Bloomsbury Publishing Plc

50 Bedford Square   1385 Broadway
London   New York
WC1B 3DP   NY 10018
UK   USA

www.bloomsbury.com

BLOOMSBURY and the Diana logo are trademarks of Bloomsbury Publishing Plc

First published in Great Britain 2014
This paperback edition first published in 2015

British Library Cataloguing-in-Publication Data
A catalogue record for this book is available from the British Library.

ISBN: HB: 978-1-4088-1599-1
       PB: 978-1-4088-3537-1
       ePub: 978-1-4088-3536-4

2 4 6 8 10 9 7 5 3 1

Typeset by Hewer Text UK Ltd, Edinburgh
Printed and bound in Great Britain by CPI Group (UK) Ltd, Croydon CR0 4YY

MIX
Paper from
responsible sources
FSC® C020471

To find out more about our authors and books visit www.bloomsbury.com.
Here you will find extracts, author interviews, details of forthcoming
events and the option to sign up for our newsletters.

For Nellie

There will be deep play tonight at Marybone, and consequently money may be pick'd up upon the road.

Macheath, in John Gay's *The Beggar's Opera*

PART ONE

AUTUMN 2007

Chapter One

FRESH DECK OF CARDS

Pete was the last white man standing in Southall. He liked to say that he left school with a ripped blazer and a kick up the arse. The reality was not so dramatic, but he had endured bullying at school for being smelly and clinically obese. The reason he was smelly was because his mother had left him with his three-year-old sister and a violent, alcoholic father when he was six months old. So sometimes he felt entitled to be dramatic. When I met him, he was thirty-nine years old, six foot four, and as slim and willowy as a drainpipe that has become unattached from a wall. He still looked young enough to turn the charm on, skinny enough to slink his way up to the bar and order a drink for the 'ladies'. Pink pouches under his eyes and a tired leer gave the game away by the time the drink had done the damage. This was how he appeared to me as he hovered over me in the pub where I found him. A late-teenage attack of meningitis had cured him of obesity. Two years in the Army in Belfast had given him a lean torso and self-assurance. But the stretch marks were still there, a reminder of childish scoffing on fast foods, sugary drinks and anything else he could get his hands on. I knew how he felt: as a child and into adulthood I liked to eat food with no structure, no beginning or end: nursery food, puddings, rice and pasta, packets of biscuits and entire Swiss rolls in order to fill the void within myself. I recognised Pete as my kindred spirit the moment I saw him.

It was September 2007 and I had moved to Southall, having bought a long blue narrowboat moored on a private dock on the Grand Union Canal. The scene was so charming I handed over a cheque and struck the deal. I like to move quickly. Once installed, I realised I had made a familiar mistake. I couldn't get basic equipment to work, and I was so overwhelmed by the basics of life I could do nothing about it. At least there was a cat flap in the rear cabin, and the cats were enjoying hunting dragonflies. In 2007 my answer to life's challenges was oblivion. So I located the likeliest-looking lad in the dodgiest-looking dive I could find. Within half an hour he had confirmed my initial suspicions – he had a bag of skunk, which is a solid foundation for any relationship. He also had a plausibility that wrapped itself around me in a comforting haze. By the end of the night, he was my boyfriend.

He was full of hatred. He hated Bozzos, Bindis, Scots, Micks and fat people, blacks, Pakis, Punjabis, bed-wetters, junkies, pill-heads, crack-heads and wife-beaters, because-I'm-worth-it babes, happy people, call-centre workers, the DHSS and the police. Most of all, he hated his mother, and the girl who had been the love of his life, and who had betrayed him. Pete hated so many people he had no one to turn to and nowhere to go except among the people he hated the most – those closest to him. They made him feel better about himself, because they were further down the road of self-destruction. I knew how he felt. I knew why he could not leave them.

This was what I had come to after a lifetime of running away. I was born to an English mother, and my Italian father left when I was twelve. We had already been round the world and back again. I was educated at great cost to save me from the destitution my parents had known. War babies do not forget their hardships. Money was thrown at me, and I was lost, confused and bewildered. I started stealing. Before that, it had been gambling, but I knew I could not win at that game. The bank always wins. Ask any casino manager. At twelve, I took my first drug. I enjoyed the violence and crime that went with it. I enjoyed some success as a writer. But I could not stay away from my drugs. I found myself on a leaky boat, at my wit's end, in Southall. I had just one thing going for me. I could write.

Southall is an island. Once you get here, it's hard to leave. If you're patient and determined, the 607 bendy bus will take you from Uxbridge Road to White City. But you have to be patient.

I had returned like a bird swooping through the woods to her mother's childhood home although my mother had long since left it. I returned through a grime of empty glasses. I walked strange streets – Orchard Street, The Broadway, Bridge Road – in which markets and cafés burst with foreign life. I myself was a ghost, or a bird, confining myself to shyness, rarely moving from cover. I moved to Southall because I had nowhere left to go. I lived on a boat on the canal, and I walked the towpath into town. I was tempted by the glazed cakes displayed like crayons in the windows of Indian restaurants, and the golden dome on top of a temple. This parade of colours reminded me of my mother's promises of sweetness. I was tempted, too, by the forlorn drifts of smokers outside one of the last public houses in this forgotten outpost of London. Their grey, defeated faces reminded me of my mother's sadness.

I could not stop staring at them and I did not know why. All I knew was that Orchard Street was singing a couple of deals before dawn and there were life lessons to be learnt from shopping on The Broadway. I was hooked, and then I found my connection. On the corner of Orchard Street, where it turns into Shackleton Road, stood the Brickmakers' Arms, and standing by the bar, glowing like a nuclear core, stood Pete, an unusually tall white man in Southall.

The Brickmakers' was a place where people had stopped caring about themselves. This was why I liked it. It was a rackety old pub with dingy carpets, cracked windows and smoke-stained walls, a jukebox, a pool table and a satellite dish. The landlord, 'Babbu', was a round smiley face of a man with an orange turban and a beard dyed a shade of Tango to match. He seemed to be in a permanent state of semi-consciousness that helped him overlook the obvious signs of illicit activities. There was a lot of receiving going on and a fair bit of pimping. Pete was his favourite customer. Babbu was old school and respected the white man, Pete avowed. However, he also admitted that Babbu liked Pete's money and he easily spent a score in the Brickmakers' each night. Pete was a rarity in Southall: a man who could buy his own and other people's drinks. He kept a close eye on his tab, though, and all the while was keeping count of money going out and his return on it. Similarly, Babbu's sleepy eyes belied his business acumen. He owned the Brickmakers' and several shops on Orchard Street. It was rumoured, as it was about most businesses in Southall, that the Brickmakers' was a front for nefarious doings. This made it all the more compelling that I take my place here at the bar, drinking cheap vodka and slimline tonic. Babbu understood his clientele. No wine was served here. The spirits were rudimentary. They did the job, and that was the point of them. I liked getting to the point.

Pete was unbeatable at this game. After each heavyweight bout in the Brickmakers', followed by afters at the Harvester in bucolic Norwood Green, he strutted home along the towpath admiring the narrowboats and the night skies, dispensing wisdom to late-night stragglers, one jaunty shoulder roll after another, to lay his head to rest in the hell he called home.

You would never guess it, but there was a siding to the canal that cut through Shackleton Estate and Newlocks Estate into the bowels of a factory. The abundance of water, trees, finches and ducks on this slip of a dock entranced me. At the end of the towpath, where the boats got more battered, their owners less proud, was a large pool that was once the loading area for Monsted's Maypole Dairy, a margarine factory. It was dead water now, overlooked by a new factory. Its workers churned out the world's supply of Sugar Puffs. Southall gives rise to the Honey Monster. I remembered him from my childhood: 'Where's the honey, Mummy?' though I never ate his product. My mother looked down on anything that wasn't Special K. Sugar Puffs operatives worked night shifts. In the darkness, floor to ceiling windows blazed with light for several storeys; the walls fizzed with machinery. In the stillness of the dock in the brambles and scramble of boats to see that factory buzzing and sparking as though fit to bust – the noise of whirring production lines and pounders and grinders was captivating. I could smell the molasses in the morning. I could hear the tap-tap-tapping of swans working their beaks along the side of my boat to scrape the algae deposited by the canal. I loved this place. It was made for rhapsody.

After Monsted's margarine and before the Honey Monster, it was Quaker Oats. Alongside the dock, Quaker Lane sidled round Shackleton Estate as though scared of making inroads through the middle. The concrete pragmatism of the estate left my rural cut behind me like a dream. The alleyways had their fair share of hoodies, but no abandoned trollies, overgrown gardens, or graffiti. It was an impressively well-maintained sink estate; its largely Punjabi residents taking care of appearances. Pete explained that Shackleton was council and Newlocks was housing association. This meant that Shackleton Estate housed older immigrants and the few remaining white families in Southall and Newlocks housed Somalis and the occasional Bosnian. The two estates were at war, and only the dock divided them.

I wanted to see what those who went before me could see and what those who lived alongside me were hiding. I looked out of my porthole into the green mirror of the canal and this was what I could see: the brick fields of Middlesex, the dock and the margarine factory, riots and the Hambrough Tavern. Closer to home, on Southall Green, outside the Tudor Manor House, young Somalis in grey hoods were selling shots for tenners. I liked these boys. They were polite to me. I chewed khat with them in the back of take-away shacks. Then I listened to Pete's boys bitch about them over my pint of Magnum's cider in the pub. It was all about territory. The Somalis did their shotting in the Manor grounds, and outside the Tudor Rose Club. 'Shotting' is slang for selling drugs on the streets. Underneath their hoods, their faces were deadpan. It was a privilege if they dropped their masks or made eye contact. They might do so for regulars, but then again they might not. It all depended. Sheena got on with her Somali dealers, but then Sheena was the Queen of the Brickmakers'.

'You're the pretty one,' they would concede when she approached, clucking, with her tenner. 'Clucking' is slang for withdrawing from opiates and crack. She was buying white because she was off brown and on a script for methadone. She was one of the few still-viable working girls in Southall. On the whole, they were not a pretty sight. Sheena was tall, and, while she stayed off the brown, she blossomed. Her cheekbones found their way up her face again. Her eyes resumed normal activity. When she got back on it, you could see her face being swamped with the drudgery of her addiction. Her body sagged again. Four births and lack of aftercare made their presence felt. Like all the girls, and on one occasion, Pete, there were signs of herpes on her lips. I had to wonder about Pete.

I thought I was different from the others. But I wasn't, and this was what hurt me. I came to Southall because it stripped away at my veneer. I came for a reason and a year later I had to leave. But there's a force at work here and I keep coming back. I found the truth here although I could not see it. I thought I was a blue-winged jay, just visiting, part of the crow family, but harder to see. If you look at Southall Green, Orchard Street, or the railway station, you'll see what I saw, a kind of beauty: a garden by the railway station in honour of the railway's dead, a vibrancy on Orchard Street that has nothing to do with diversity; a Tudor mansion on the Green that takes me back to my beginnings. People come to this island from all over. Freshies come straight off the paddy fields to work for cash and send it back home. Small brown men with cloudy eyes and no English are dumped on street corners to wait for trucks to take them to building sites. You can see them each morning if you're up early enough. And you can see them coming back to Southall each night. The police clock them, too. These small brown men are packed cheek by jowl into rows of crumbling terraced houses by their fat brown masters. These are the houses my white underclass ancestors lived in. Now it's the Beemer Boys who run the show in Southall.

'Boys are overindulged in Hindu culture,' says my interpreter, my god of the wastelands. 'Beemer Boys are the eldest sons who stay at home to look after their parents. They get an allowance to study Business or IT; they get a BMW or a rags-to-riches Merc. You can see them outside the temple, sitting in their cars doing coke, dope, crack, whatever. They live in their cars so they can keep using. One guy I know, though, he doesn't bother pretending. He keeps his pipe under the sofa, and his mum hoovers round it. He serves it up, too. Outside the house he stands by the gate, knocking out bags all day. His family's going in and out the front door – they know what's going on – but no one says anything. As long as they don't bring dishonour by leaving home, Beemer Boys can do what they like. So they do their gangster thing and take Mum shopping.'

I was brought to my knees here. But still I return to this island, this outpost, Punjabi town, Somali town, white underclass town with its strange shops selling strange things and restaurants that make Brick Lane look like Westfield. There's no such chicanery in Southall.

This is why I was here, and then I was lured further into the game of Southall by a tall white man who stood over me in the darkest pub I could find. He reminded me of my mother. Or was it my father? Amidst the smog and the fumes, all I could see were green-blue eyes and a confiding smile. That had to be my mother.

I invited him to my boat on a siding on the Grand Union Canal that slicked between Newlocks Estate and Shackleton, the estate on which he lived and which I wanted to explore for reasons as yet unknown to me. All I knew was that I could not stop myself. My curiosity was turning proverbial.

Chapter Two

LIVEABOARD

The Maypole branch of the Grand Union Canal, built in 1912 to serve the largest manufacturer of margarine in Europe, was now my home. A daisy chain of around twenty boats moored alongside a wilderness of willow trees and hedgerows had seduced me. As well as the charm of the dock, memories of my great-uncle Danny's chain of Pound shops on The Broadway added to the allure. For the brief span of the 1970s Great-uncle Danny was King of Southall. But the canal and the railway opened Southall up to global influences, from Maypole Dairy margarine and Quaker Oats, through to Patak's Curry Sauces, Heathrow Airport and Sugar Puffs. Danny's businesses faltered, as did my family's fortunes. I was determined to rekindle them and as autumn turned from rusty red to wilted brown, I coaxed and cajoled the stubborn spirit of regeneration to do its work. I had found myself in a corner of London full of arcane treasures: fertile meadows, burnt-out vans, abandoned factories, fully functioning factories, industrial estates framed with brick arches and laced with internal waterways, winding lanes, stretches of woodland and struggling streams that plotted their way back to the River Thames. I had found my slice of history, caked in countryside. I could see

Bixley Fields, where the bricks for Buckingham Palace were once made, from my galley porthole. On that first day it seemed as though here I could find anything I set my heart on. By the close of autumn, one thing had certainly been made clear. I had heard it said that boatyards are where divorced men come to die. I could vouch for that. I was in retreat from middle-aged concerns and realities. So I set myself the task of becoming invisible. In so doing, I burrowed deep beneath the earth in order to embark on a series of discoveries.

I started a sketch of a family tree commencing with my birth in 1965. At this stage, the tree was more of a sapling. My mother, Greta Ann, née Kingham, was a thirty-two-year-old baccalaureate secretary possessed of a need for respectability that was to leave me cold around the age of twelve. I could not find the warmth I needed from her because she was hard at work earning a living and holding her head high. Similarly my father, an Italian émigré, had never really been available for comment. So I had to make the painful choice of leaving him as he had once left me. His side of the family drew a blank, and I needed love from somewhere so I moved up a level. The next perch was my maternal grandmother, my namesake. But Lilian née Kingham had a marked preference for the male of the species and addressed herself fully to their chaotic lifestyle choices. It is safe to say that her son's heroin addiction and his father's criminal manoeuvrings left her helpless and sorrowful and an object of pity rather than a pioneering female adventurer – the woman I wanted to be. Her sister, however, my great-aunt Dolly, was a woman altogether more original in her approach to the game of life, and I was getting warmer. My sapling was now leaning to the left as I plotted out Dolly's progress from the cradle. I became absorbed in my task as I felt I was getting close to some shattering revelation. My fingers tingled with it as I pencilled in the names of my long-gone forebears, my great-grandparents, Daniel Kingham and Emily-Elsie Smith.

First, I pinched my left nostril and felt a tingly, burning sensation flow into my sinuses and a bitter taste in my throat, and all of a sudden, all those wretched feelings – wanting something but having no idea what it was, thinking it was sex and then realising it wasn't because of the guilt and what happened before; all that wandering and wondering that made me see myself as some kind of derelict; that agony of drinking and drinking and not getting drunk and nothing being resolved and no one understanding, least of all myself; and no peace at all except when I was writing or reading or playing with my cats; and then the minute my mind stopped me writing, reading or playing with my cats the continual, insistent search resumed just so that I could get home again, pass out and come round in the morning and say to myself, 'Oh God, not another day of this, please.' So I get up and vomit so that I can start again – but then, all of a sudden, all of a sudden, the demons and the jeering voices and the wandering and the wondering, all the petty frustrations and the deep rage vanished and they didn't exist at all because I felt powerful. That was cocaine.

As my family tree grew branches, a distraction emerged in the elegant shape of a young black woman in a tailored wool coat and court shoes. I spotted her through my porthole and couldn't help but watch this tall and pouting semi-supermodel trailing a fake Louis Vuitton case on wheels. Something caught her attention, she turned round, and spotted me following her progress up the towpath. She smirked, shrugged a shoulder and carried on regardless, although perhaps there was a more studied smoothness to the swing of her hips. At the far end of the dock, which widened into the loading-bay that had once fed the factory, she moved on to a doll-sized wooden tug with all the grace of a gazelle. The boat, *Tempest*, was the smallest and prettiest on the dock. I could hear her chugging past me in the night as she steered the length of the dock and made for the entrance to the canal, turning right for old Southall and Norwood Green. What was she doing here? What brought her here? I asked my neighbours. 'Her name is Nancy, and *Tempest* belongs to her husband,' I was told. 'He met her in Ghana.' The smiles that followed were left unexplained.

When I approached her, Nancy was the epitome of grace and good manners. She almost bowed when I introduced myself by the gate of the dock.

'My name is Nancy.' Her frank and open friendliness felt like sunshine.

'You have a nice smile,' she simpered, her brilliant black eyes opening wider. I knew there was more to come.

I could say I was here because a Gypsy at a horse fair told my fortune. I was looking for a solution to life's struggles – a journey to a happy end. I wanted to be free of monthly mortgage repayments, accumulating credit card debts and a decreasing appetite for employment. I was thoroughly jaded. I had reviewed so many books for so many newspapers I felt that I was drowning in publishers' blurbs. Despite the cheerful productivity of the book industry, I yawned at the prospect of more of the same. Whatever I was going through was not being addressed by contemporary fiction. Books by women were written by a certain kind of woman speaking a certain kind of language. I came from a long line of women who did not possess an education. By the time they did, they still had not progressed to having a sense of entitlement to a voice. My mother took me to tea at our local department store, but she pretended to be someone else.

'Mmm, cucumber sandwiches,' she purred too loudly, looking around the room with bright eyes seeking out like-minded shoppers and embarrassing me into sullen silence. 'Aren't they yummy? Lily! Aren't they yummy?'

'You will cross water to find your home.' Pale green eyes set in an unlined, unsmiling face held my gaze and conveyed her seriousness. I took this woman literally, assessed the financial implications. I would release a significant amount of cash in capital by selling my flat – enough to buy the boat and live on for a year. And so I made a calculated risk that masked surrender. What I didn't realise was that the beginnings and endings I desired mimicked the finality of a whodunit narrative, and they left me stranded with my desire for resolution, and thus compelled me to begin again. Another volume of Miss Marple, another TV adaptation of Poirot, another denouement in the front parlour of a vicarage or the carriage of a steam train bound for the Orient. Another line of cocaine.

My cocaine dealer before Southall lived in Kensal Green, another stop on the Grand Union Canal. He was not a good advertisement for his product – being wild-eyed and dishevelled and too paranoid to speak. The first time I bought cocaine from him (not the first time I used it), I got through the door of my flat only to pass out in the bathroom. I cut my head open on the handle of the bathroom door on the way down to the laminated flooring. I came round a few hours later in a pool of blood. Nothing, not even wounds to the head, bloodshed and concussion, could stop my insatiable need for power. A week later I went back to the dealer for more cocaine. This time I woke up in sheets soiled with shit.

A further discovery: I had an almost obsessive preoccupa-
tion with the word 'shit'. Living on a boat meant that I had
to deal with it.

Nancy laughed at my struggles with the shit detail. 'I just
pee on the towpath if I feel like it!' I saw her one night
oblivious to passers-by, crouching in the bushes to relieve
herself before trotting off to a nightclub on her spindly heels.

My seventy-foot narrowboat was called *Adam Bonny*, and sat
low in snake-green, oily water. My nearest neighbours aft
and stern were *Evening Star* and *Bob-A-Buoy*. All three boats
were moored in companionable silence. I preferred it when
their occupants stayed aboard leaving me alone to bathe in
the air of the dock, enjoying the hush of surrounding fields,
and the hum of planes from Heathrow. But I was interrupted
by snatches of gossip drifting down the canal.

The nocturnal comings and goings of *Tempest* continued
to constitute a mystery. Nancy was proving herself to be an
excellent bargewoman. Whereas the men made heavy
weather of leaks and electrics, standing around waving span-
ners and scratching chins, Nancy's tinkling laughter fuelled
her jaunts along the canal.

'Nothing gets to her,' I sighed.

'She's young,' sighed *Bob-A-Buoy* in sympathy. He placed
a letter before me. We met regularly to plot against the dock
owner, who was extorting higher rents with threats of
enforced removals.

'The owner? He's a little man,' scoffed Nancy. 'He needs
to feel powerful,' and off she strutted on more important
business. 'I have a hair appointment in Ealing.'

Periodically, this little man who owned the dock would
patrol it with two large minders and sighing reminders that

rents were due to rise. It was his sighs that irked me – as though he regretted his voracity. More news infiltrated my isolation. Barney the coalman had changed his delivery day to Tuesdays. *My Fair Lady* and *Flying Cloud* had been burgled, the dock owner appealed to for increased security – and no response. A residents' association was formed. This was the impetus I needed. Nautical Rachmans are purpose-built to stoke my engine. A meeting was held; I attended, and alongside my neighbour *Bob-A-Buoy, Adam Bonny* was identified as being fearless. *Bob-A-Buoy* and *Adam Bonny* were duly voted Joint Chairs. *Dreadnought* made a drunken pass at *My Fair Lady*. *Bob-A-Buoy* and *Adam Bonny* drafted the minutes of the meeting. It was noted that *Adam Bonny* had developed a list. In the larger world, Southall horse market on The Broadway had been closed. Every Wednesday morning for hundreds of years, nags had been driven along Uxbridge Road to their destiny as cat meat. Not Brunel, not the factories, not even the five waters of the Punjab could stop Travellers trading in knackered horses. It was *Bob-A-Buoy* who mourned the market's demise. But it was *Bob-A-Buoy* who pointed out that the Travellers had taken their horses elsewhere. I could hear them calling out the prices every night on Bixley Fields.

Evening Star worried me. He was permanently drunk and permanently leering at no one and everyone who passed him by. It was worse when he was leering at no one but unbearable when he was leering at me. *Evening Star* longed for company and yet repulsed it. He sat atop his boat swigging from a hip flask and playing with bits of junk iron and stray wires. Every morning we would argue over the water tap that fed both our boats but was attached to the pipe in his yard. He would turn it off in order to run tests on his plumbing system, but, really, I conjectured, because he had nothing else to do. I was convinced his endless acts of 'handyman-ism' were unconsciously motivated by a need for attention. They certainly forced me into conversing with him. This put a strain on my dwindling supply of good nature. Unlike my neighbour, I was very much in touch with unconscious motivation and I was barely concealing my hostility. I resented *Evening Star*'s proximity to me, his loneliness – which gave me an unflattering reflection of my own – his intrusions on my privacy and his control over my water supply. I was beginning to see the enormity of what I had done in moving on to a boat that needed daily repair when I could not change a light bulb without a quivering attack of anxiety.

Adam Bonny had a plumbing system that consisted of a pump, a battery and strands of wire that were coated in frayed plastic. They led to a box at the back of a cupboard. The box was held together with sticky black plastic and stickers displaying skulls indicating imminent death. I needed help – *Evening Star* wanted to help but his lopsided leer and dependence on his hip flask alarmed me. I turned to *Bob-A-Buoy*. He gave me a phone number. Buster was a bargee of many years' standing and I paid him to show me how to live aboard. I felt more comfortable with a financial arrangement even though he insisted on telling me stories about barge life, his own life, his daughter's career in office management and her new boyfriend's bad knee. I had enough on my mind without having to share the ups and downs of Buster's extended family. In fact, I worked hard to avoid the intricacies of relationships in order to maintain solitude in order not to be driven mad.

*   *   *

The mornings were steadily greeting me with pitch black –
the steel case to my boat conducted the cold of the water,
and my electric duvet was faulty. Even if her blessing was to
bring about resurgence, the curse of *Adam Bonny* was to cause
malfunction. I woke at five to stoke the oven with coals, bits
of bracken and lighter fuel. I boiled a kettle on the one gas
hob that worked. I had mastered the plumbing and by the
time I had drawn a bath the boat was toasty. I left for work at
six, relishing this hitherto unknown realm of early morning
commuters (we greeted each other with rueful smiles), the
clusters of stars, traffic muted as though in mourning and
wisps of cloud and mist stroking my face. The journey from
Southall to HMP Chelmsford was epic, emerging from
underground to overground and rosy dawn. There were
significant stretches on foot across light industry and woodland surrounding the River Chelmer. I never thought I could
enjoy travelling to work in the mornings. I was too rebellious
to 'join in'. But for the first time in my life I had found a
purpose and I was happy to be like everyone else. I had found
a place where I felt needed. Unfortunately, I could not ignore
for much longer that I had needs of my own.

After the long journey home and over *Bob-A-Buoy*'s recipe
for Bargees' Stew, I gleaned what I could from my family tree.
The trunk was gaining sturdy branches that took me down
the Grand Union Canal to its resting place at Paddington
Basin. According to their marriage certificate this was where
my father was lodging when he met my mother. I was tracing
resemblances. While Pino Pizzichini was now on the other
side of the world working in the casino trade managing punters, I was on the other side of London managing prisoners.
The great thing about prisoners is that they cannot leave you.
I kept returning, as though in a hall of mirrors, to my father,

from whom I inherited a love of adrenalin surges, the intoxication of power, and who left me. I lived with this abandonment as though it were the family silver that I took out every now and again to polish. Others saw me differently.

'You're a motivator,' my colleagues said. 'You inspire the men.'

I wanted to empower working-class criminals to become writers and to occupy spheres of influence. I did good work but I was undermined by a hidden agenda. What I did not realise was that my addiction was managing me.

With the exception of weekend trips to the dreaded sluice, which I undertook at twilight when no one was about, I pursued withdrawal with a vengeance. But the chemical toilet demanded commando-style missions. When drinking and using drugs on a daily basis, after a few years paranoia sets in. It signals detachment from the human race. I am no longer one of you, and it is imperative you do not discover my alien status. It became crucial to the success of my mission that no one saw me. If someone did and they said 'hello', I must deter any further advances. I wore a hooded anorak as though it were a magic cloak that conferred invisibility. Curtains drawn and portholes covered, I removed the sloshing cartridge from the edifice of the toilet, and placed it in a wheelbarrow with a broken wheel. I then dragged it up the towpath, terrified the barrow would skid and catapult its contents into the canal. If one of the divorcees stuck his head out of a cabin door, I nodded grimly. They got the hint. Boatyards are full of loners and their recycling bins are full of bottles.

Once I reached the sluice, I unscrewed the lid of the cartridge, emptied it, flushed it out with a bright-blue chemical wash, and gained an understanding of the consequences of producing waste material. I grew used to the rhythms of mundane existence. I felt quite comfortable with paranoia and enjoyed being alone with my cats on a boat watching birds feed on seeds and leaves fall. I felt closer to the earth and to a source of light and darkness because, again, light was something I could not take for granted. The 'electrics' on the dock were constantly 'tripping'. Resolving the situation involved a highly complex operation involving a spanner and a torch that I never got to grips with. Instead, I waited for one of the neighbours to grope their way through the dark and tackle the fuse box so that I could be restored to a semblance of sanity. The television was my mainstay and support. When the aerial faltered as it often did – 'atmospheric pressure', commiserated *Bob-A-Buoy* – I would be reduced to dry, heaving sobs until normal service was resumed.

Some mornings, I woke up and groaned at the prospects of what had to be done that day. I was weary to the core and my joints were on strike. But every six weeks I would force myself to take the long walk to the bus stop and mount the bendy bus to Ealing Broadway. This was a sophisticated metropolis – Marks & Spencer, a shopping plaza and Costa. Here I masqueraded as a mature but attractive female intellectual drinking caffè latte. There was a distinctly Eastern European feel to the cafés of Ealing that gave me room to breathe. I felt I was on holiday. But staying seated too long caused my joints to seize. As I hoisted myself into an upright position, I did not feel so attractive. The only answer was lipstick, a 'dash-it-all' attitude and a glass of wine. At some point in the early evening, the large expanse of sky that presided over Southall gave me some peace.

With *Evening Star* safely stowed in his shed, muttering over spare parts, I stood on the sloping foredeck of *Adam Bonny* and enjoyed the distant noises of Orchard Street diffused by a shimmering sky and the aroma of wood burning in neighbours' stoves.

Winter was approaching. Pete came round one night to smoke some heroin.

'Nice and shipshape,' he said bending double to enter through the hatch and into the galley kitchen. At six foot four Pete was unable to stand upright in the boat. He had to stoop which suited his cotton-bud frame and my desire for protection. Pete had innocent opaque eyes and the mouth of a charmer. It helped that he was carrying some class A drugs that produced a seductive, cosseting warmth that made all life's struggles evaporate, and situations from which others would shrink fine and dandy.

Heroin is like when the black girls at school 'rel-a-a-x-ed' their hair. It took me back to the adverts in Brixton beauty parlours with their bright colours and soothing lotions and being ministered to by shiny angels with relaxed curls.

'What's a nice middle-class girl like you doing slumming it on a leaky old boat in Southall?' I liked the way Pete got to the point with unerring precision. Class was an issue wherever I went. When I did find a position where others had more diverse backgrounds (the subs' desk), I wasn't tough enough. I overheard the editor demanding more 'cunt' stories, and I heard the chief sub comment on my breasts. Outraged at this male efflorescence, I flounced out in my skintight T-shirt with no bra. At the *Times Literary Supplement*, I was an editorial assistant, which meant opening packages containing new books and typing their ISBNs into a database. At first I enjoyed cutting through cardboard with a Stanley knife. However, inputting the data was tedium, like being crucified but without the pain. There were many friendly, talented writers working at the *TLS*, whose books I had stacked on the shelves of a bookshop – my first job after leaving university. I was overawed. My desk abutted the tea trolley and fax machine. My stellar colleagues gathered under my nose to engage in witty banter and fax A. S. Byatt, while waiting for the kettle to boil. I opened my mouth and I couldn't even whistle.

If I could not find my niche here it was because I was seeking the comfort (and inspiration) of a complementary narrative. Julie Burchill didn't do it for me. She was too self-consciously money-minded. I wanted to have money without having to work for it. When Irvine Welsh's *Trainspotting* was published, I spotted my chance to have my say. But another colleague, a young Old Etonian, spotted it also. He not only read the book, he saw the stage adaptation and then the film. He could not get enough of Welsh's wild style, so much so that he had to appropriate it and make it his own. I wanted to tell him that I, too, felt the thrill, that I had come from somewhere like this godforsaken place and was heading relentlessly towards it. But I baulked in the wake of his striding confidence, which, once again, stoked the fuel of my class resentment. There's that sense of entitlement again, and it isn't mine.

I told Pete about my great-aunt Dolly whose spirit was beginning to haunt me. Dolly was my reason for coming here, I said. In 1968, and again in 1975, Dolly was subjected to electro-convulsive therapy. 'They didn't give her the benefit of the couch,' Pete guffawed.

But, more important, I flourished the piece of paper on which I was gathering fruit for my family tree. Dolly lived just off Southall Broadway during the war! With her mother

Emily-Elsie and her brother Danny! Pete did not share my excitement.

I wondered if I was seeking revenge. I wondered if it was anger that drove my great-aunt insane, and caused doctors to do insane things to her in the name of medical competence, and if the same would happen to me.

'Better out than in,' Dolly used to say. But she wasn't talking about self-expression or channelling anger; she was talking about wind and its proper distribution. It doesn't matter. Either way, she was right. It's all shit in the end. It seemed a natural progression to smoke heroin with a retired burglar.

Pete opened the wrap, dark brown powder – a dense, gooey resin, 'a vast improvement on the stuff you get round here', because Pete had connections with Iranians at Heathrow. We sat side by side on my immaculate two-seater sofa opposite my shiny Squirrel stove, coals glimmering. I gave magazine living an edge. For the purposes of my night in with my new boyfriend, I had provided ashtrays, lighters and foil. He tore off a sheet, rolled it into a tube so that he could burn the bottom of the foil so that the powder would turn into liquid so that we could inhale the fumes. Opiates depress the central nervous system. A warm breeze washed over me. The light from the coals brightened. Up close Pete had begun to look gaunt and shadowy. Now he was looking more wholesome. There was music in the air. Despite the fact that educationally and culturally we were poles apart, we were both swimming upstream in the Ready Brek glow that is the immediate effect of smoking heroin.

'The best time to commit a burglary is two or three in the morning when everyone's out on a thank-fuck-it's-Friday bender. I tend to wait for rainy nights so that I can break a window. Rain deadens the sound. You're very much aware when you're on a job; your senses are heightened. Adrenalin is coursing through you; you're listening for any sound, any sign of life. When I'm on a job, I'm a hundred and ten per cent *on* and I'm on top of the game. I'll look around with my torch, the usual places, the nooks and crannies, ever vigilant. I'll creep up the stairs. If I'm aware they're creaking, I'll step back a moment.'

Like a pantomime villain, he arched his back and lifted his leg in the air, miming indecision. This was no mean feat in a ten foot by six galley.

'What to do now? . . . Take them two at a time . . . Gloves are on.'

He smoothed gloves over pliant fingers, and sat back down again.

'PVC is preferable, but depending on the weather a thin leather driving glove is good. I don't want to get caught with Marigolds or anything suspicious. Picking ornaments up' – his long arms ranged across me towards the shelves bearing books and papers – nothing of any value there – 'going through drawers and cabinets, looking in kitchen cupboards where people store cash in biscuit tins and jam jars. I'd find a roll of cash and say to myself: right, this is a start; let's get on with it.'

As he reminisced he could not help looking round the cabin, scanning the shelves for signs of saleable items, guessing at the contents of my tea canister and biscuit barrel. His gaze was swift, cursory and left no stone unturned. I understood the rapacious nature of his curiosity. It wasn't just their seeming smoothness I desired. I wanted what they had, the abundance of possessions, cars, car alarms, children, schools, executive salaries, high-level decisions, picture bylines and cashmere throws. By now I knew something was missing. I thought someone else had it instead of me, and it wasn't fair.

I suspected Pete felt similarly, only he did something about it.

'What if there's someone in, and you disturb them?' I asked.

His answer was matter-of-fact. 'You have to take charge. If it's a couple I'll go to the woman and use her as a bargaining tool. I'll threaten the woman with extreme violence, either with or without a knife, to subdue the husband. I have to see if he wants to be a hero or not. Usually, I'll make my preparations in advance and find out who exactly is in the house because I don't want children waking up and making a fuss. The best thing to do is go prepared: with masking tape, with extra sets of rubber gloves, ropes, Stanley knives, butcher's knives, carving knives, hammers. Those little plastic ties are good: you just slip them round the wrists and ankles, and they're immobilised. You want them immobilised.'

My mind was racing with startling images – a bedroom, the darkness, a couple in their nightclothes – her in a silk slip, him in pyjama bottoms, maybe a vest. This man, Pete but not Pete, this man must be a stranger. (In a balaclava? I'd have to ask him later.)

He paused so that we could refuel. The images dissolved, and 'rel-a-a-x' washed over me making what was unacceptable seem quite reasonable. I sat back for more.

'The important thing is not to panic because that's when accidents happen – I'll call them accidents because that's the user-friendly term.'

'You like to be in control,' I said. Whether I was in or out of a heroin trance, I thought I had a handle on Pete and that I could open him up that little bit further. 'How do you keep control without hurting someone?'

'You tell the guy to lie down, face on the floor, hands behind his back, just like the police would say. "Otherwise

I'm going to fucking seriously hurt this woman." I found towards the end people started protesting more. I put it down to them going to the gym and that . . . standing up for their rights and all that.

'The last burglary I did was late one night just past Bixley Fields, going towards the Brent River. I'd been pottering around in someone's garden – there's some nice properties backing on to the allotments. I found a key in a garden shed. It had been left there for the builders the next day. I opened the patio door, got into the house, crept up the stairs. They were creaking. I got to the top. A bedroom door opened. A naked man came walking across the corridor towards me. He looked at me, and went into the toilet. A couple of minutes later, he came out again and walked straight past me. I thought I'd better leave before he realised he wasn't dreaming.'

Pete was a creeper. When I was burgled (three times in deepest, darkest Hackney), I became too frightened to leave the house until I could buy my way out. I got a mortgage on a flat on the Kensal Green branch of the Grand Union Canal where I found that dodgy product. My nice little flat backed on to the famous cemetery. Dolly had also lived in a nice little flat here. She and Danny set up house together although Dolly paid for everything. Then he left her to go back to Southall and she lost the flat on a bet. I lost my flat because I could not keep up with the bills cascading through my letterbox, and because I had become so overwhelmed by the technicalities of adult life, I became a victim of crime again. Domestic violence. I was escaping shame and debt when I moved to Southall. But my logic got warped along the way. Victims are collateral damage, and I was determined not to become a victim again. Who better to aid me than a tooled-up burglar?

The morning light reminded me of impending withdrawals. But the clawing anxiety was leavened by shivering thrills. I was being admitted entrance to a club not full of cashmere throws and savings accounts but equally exclusive and mindful of its contents. This time I had found an inhabitant who was willing to reveal some closely guarded secrets. He chose the right person. He told me what happened to the man and the woman in the picture, and heroin, and the heaviness inside me, made it OK.

'A good tie to take on a job is a nylon rope cut into reasonable lengths. I'd secure her hands behind her back and then her legs at the ankles. Once she was immobilised, I'd make my way over to him; stand on his neck or put my knee into the centre of his back, tie his hands up, do his feet. Then it's down to finding out what you want to know. Is there cash in the house? Where is it? What are the pin numbers to your credit cards? A few years ago, before everything was on CCTV, you could go to a cash point and come away with thousands of pounds.'

It was the advent of CCTV and constant paranoia that prompted a career rethink. Pete was no longer a burglar. I was not sure how I felt about this.

'Yes, I had to stop. I was constantly on the edge, thinking about the next move; looking for a way out – there had to be a way out – a window – not too high up – or a fire exit, and this was when I was *at home*. In the end, I had to find a new job.'

This was a shame, because I was up for doing a burglary.

Chapter Three

A FINE FELLOW

Long before I moved to Southall, in the autumn of 1939 my great-grandmother, Emily-Elsie Smith, moved into 29 Woodlands Road, just off Uxbridge Road. This was a new side to Southall, houses built in the early 1930s, the streets arranged in rows. After a lifetime of dwelling in slums, this was to be Emily-Elsie's last home. Her life is characterised by struggle and poverty. In 1926, she was widowed, left with five children. Two years later, she had another child, my great-uncle Danny. By the time she moved to Southall, Emily-Elsie was a fifty-one-year-old charwoman with one breast, a withered arm, a club foot and a soft spot for whisky. She had two adult daughters living with her, working as waitresses. So she was finally able to find some repose in her new, relatively spacious home. Number 29 was a two-up, two-down with a kitchen, outside toilet and front room. There was a back alley with access to a coal shed. There was a garden with an Anderson shelter. The day they moved in, Emily-Elsie's twelve-year-old, Danny, took occupation of it. He hid his hoard of cigarette cards, his darts and dartboard, and other random treasures, on the top bunk. He'd staked his claim.

I can picture Emily-Elsie and Dolly in their square of garden bounded by a low brick wall. This is their first garden. Emily-Elsie is tiny and dark in widow's weeds, and Dolly, in lavender grey, with emphatic red hair and rouged lips, would have joined her in surveying their new home. The Virginia creeper from next door was lending its leaves as camouflage to the Anderson. But knowing Dolly as I do, she would have been taken with the view above. The steel-blue slate of sky smudged with clouds was as large as the sea she had seen at Southend. There was not this much space or silence where she came from. As an old lady, she would take me for walks in Holland Park. We would hide behind trees, on the look-out for the park warden. Dolly's dog was off the leash, so there was an element of precaution in our ramblings – the possibility that we didn't quite belong there. But it is the blur of leaves and the rough barks of trees that I remember – the sheer weight and density of green-blue darkness. Dolly and I breathed it in. In Southall, I can feel her heart expanding in the suburban dusk. Next to her, Emily-Elsie is resolute in being downcast.

'Danny *Overton!* Danny *Overton!*' This was the taunt that drove my great-uncle away from her. Now he was back. Danny pulled the door to 29 Woodlands Road behind him. The latch clicked into place. He held his breath, waiting for the sound to subside. The leaf drop of his footfall across the threshold was barely audible. He stood statue-like, ears alert, to check for signs of his mother. The passage was dark and silent. He could not hear women snapping at each other – his mother and his sister Dolly engaged in their *pas de deux*. The absence of women's voices and the smell of bread baking in the oven beckoned him into the kitchen. The smell of baking bread was not a ploy to convey domestic comfort but an indicator that the ingredients for bread were cheap and plentiful. A chunk of it could last all day. Sometimes, a chunk of bread dipped in days-old stew was all they had. But it was something.

Danny luxuriated in being alone. It was a rare occurrence and it gave him the space he needed for his heroic imaginings. A chipped enamel teapot stood on the sideboard. He helped himself to a cup of stewed tea, and emptied his pockets. Out came his set of Chesterfield's 'Air Raid Precautions' cigarette cards. The sequence of five images told him what to do in the event of an incendiary device landing on 29 Woodlands Road. The first card showed a figure in blue overalls crawling through wreckage towards a black spiky ball. Danny closed his eyes, compressing himself into the scene: the laboured breathing, smoke and dust, blue overalls, inching his way towards imminent danger, scoop and hoe in hand. The next card showed he must clasp the device with said scoop and hoe. Keep a cowering distance. Steady under pressure. Next: direct a jet of water from a nearby hosepipe on to the device, thereby cooling it. The fourth card was not so clear. It seemed to Danny that he had to lift this solid mass of fatal explosives with the scoop and hoe and place it in a coal scuttle. The last card in the deck showed him shovelling sand on it.

He poured himself his second cup of cold brown tea. Another spoonful of sugar, because Dolly let him. She gave up her rations so quickly he hardly had time to notice. Danny turned his attention to the rusty coin on the table. He could just make out the hooked nose of an emperor.

'Coin of the realm,' said the King of the Road, as he handed it to his new young friend. The night before, Danny had had an adventure.

* * *

He had not known he was going to spend a night under the stars. All he had known was that he had to get out. He had not turned right because that meant running the gauntlet of Southall Broadway and the possibility of Dolly spotting him from the top of the trolley bus. The 607 from Shepherd's Bush brought her along Uxbridge Road to the stop at Woodlands Road at 7 p.m. each night, back from her shift at Lyons. He turned left. Stark and proud against the sky, and tinted Titian blue like the robe of a virgin was the gasometer. It rose round and resplendent on the horizon, its miraculous contents clasped inside. It was the first thing you saw on Woodlands Road as you got off the trolley bus.

Beyond the gasworks, now defunct, and to the left again, lay the hope of wastelands and wilderness and Southall's light industry. If Danny couldn't find the centre because it was always beyond his reach, and school held no challenge for him because it was learning by rote, then he sought mystery and knowledge beyond the grid of suburban streets. He turned left out of number 29 and left at the end on to Beaconsfield Road. Danny William Overton Kingham was ill at ease with boundaries, frustrated by pavements that stopped at kerbs, foxed by crossings that required a change of direction, and resentful of walls that stopped him in his tracks. He wanted the geography of his world to go on and on without stopping. He was heading for Waddy's Dump.

Southall in the early evening has the promise of Christmas. The shops are shut but they don't seem it. They are pulling you in with their promise of having it all.

On Beaconsfield Road still, Danny passed rows of houses just like his. The gasometer, at three hundred and twenty feet high, still presides over Southall. Danny's neighbours were convinced that the Luftwaffe were using it as a guide for their

bombers looking for the viaduct on Uxbridge Road. Luftwaffe maps show the gasometer highlighted. The year after
Danny and his family moved in, a hundred and twenty-six
high explosives as well as hundreds of incendiary bombs fell
on Southall. Nineteen people were killed. Woolworth's on
the high street was destroyed, its remains decanted on to
Waddy's Dump. The raggle-taggle residents of old Southall
sifted through the damaged goods.

Danny turned right on to South Road. I can see him –
tall and fair, and immediately this raises questions: where
did he get his height? The angle of his cheekbones? The
Kingham face is round and open with snubbed features.
Danny's is so angular it is almost regal. South Road leads
into old Southall, past the straggling vestiges of a Georgian
terrace, past the florid Oriental façade of the Palace Cinema,
past the now-famous Glassy Junction pub, where customers
would pay for their Cobra beer in rupees. He stopped
outside Southall Station. In 1838, Brunel's wide gauge cut
the village of Southall in two. For the first year, there was
no station, just a level-crossing gate. Now there was a coffee
stall outside, and it was doing business. The 18.32 GWR
(God's Wonderful Railway) from Paddington had just
discharged its load of commuters. Danny sheltered in the
light and heat of Mr Nelms' pitch on the bridge built over
the tracks of the railway. The view towards Hayes was
breathtaking (it still is) – all that sky and a solemn, red-brick
water tower. To Danny, it looked like the fortress containing the Count of Monte Cristo. Then there were the five
lanes of railway tracks reaching as far as Bristol, and, to the
right, the spectral gasometer.

All those nights combing the streets alone Southall had
fuelled his imaginings – it was a place of adventure because,

somehow, it seemed unfinished, always beginning and yet always emerging from a distant past.

He warmed himself by Mr Nelms' charcoal fire. Nelms was selling tea, coffee and Oxo (a large cup for 1½d) and slices of baked bread pudding, with sugar on top, cut into triangles, at 1d each. Danny wanted one. But he had no money. The white-collar commuters gathered round the stall weren't in the mood to take pity on a boy. So he moved on.

Just behind the station was the Quaker Oats factory. Hundreds of machinists were coming home for dinner. Their houses were smaller and older than Danny's – darker and damper – but still one step up from the building where he had been born, and two steps up from the building where Dolly had been born. But he didn't know about that. Not many did. He carried on towards old Southall. He turned right past the cemetery where eight years later Emily-Elsie would lie buried in a pauper's grave. I have seen the long plot of turf in Hortus Cemetery, where she and so many others are buried. A wall runs alongside it. On the other side of this wall, every time I went to the pub – and it was always at twilight – I was walking past my great-grandmother. I felt a cord tighten round my waist, pulling me back, but I couldn't stop.

Danny paused before he reached a patch of land that used to be watercress fields and that would one day become a housing estate. This is where his great-niece sits in a gutter crying into the night. She is crying because she does not know what she is doing here. Danny had reached his destination, Waddy's Dump.

It had once been Mr Waddington's pig farm. Now it was a dumping ground for refuse from bombed properties. Out-of-work machinists scavenged in the wreckage. Danny would watch them, refusing to join in. Tonight he found Alf. Caesar

came to Middlesex and so did Alf. He came by way of the
Grand Union towpath, exiting at the lock, stomping through
the fields to Waddy's Dump. Alf had once been a boatman
and he bypassed the modern and the mechanical. Now he was
sitting on a mound of ash and rubble, silhouetted against the
night, staring at an improvised fire, smoking a handmade pipe.
Around the Dump, the brown London stock houses showed
their backsides. Danny was familiar with the narrow lanes that
ran between and behind these back-to-backs. These lanes
were his main thoroughfare – the clothes lines as high as ships'
masts, the sheds filled with sacks of potatoes and turnips. He
helped himself to spuds and nips from time to time, and left
them on the kitchen table. They went in the stew.

Danny watched the man from the foothills of the Dump.
At this distance, Alf looked like a dusty old guy made from
rags. His coat and trousers were held together by string. He
wore a peaked cap, and sat on a canvas bag that bulged with
treasures. Danny made his approach.

'Hello, son,' Alf said, as though he had been waiting for him.

The embers from the fire were all the light they had.
Danny sat down and looked into a yellow face with sunken
cheeks and shadowed eyes. A weed called tramps' delight
grew in profusion here, a tall plant with thin, curly leaves.
Danny made a show of catching the smoke curling from
Alf's pipe.

'You like to smoke?'

Danny nodded.

'This is what you do.'

Alf reached into his pocket and picked out a strip of newspaper from a tobacco tin. He rolled some dried leaves into it,
and finished it off with a line of spit. He lit the roll-up from
a twig in the fire and passed it to Danny. It was nothing like

Dolly's Woodbines, but Danny liked pretending that nothing was new. Alf ignored his spluttering.

'It was just the other day,' he said, 'that I was thinking of very old times, when Southall was covered in forest. When the Romans first came here. Two thousand years ago. And then, just now, I found this.' He held up a tiny black coin. Danny had a feeling that sitting here high above Southall he was in for the long haul. He settled down among the ashes, and listened.

'Before the Angles and the Saxons arrived, there were Roman soldiers here – some of them came from North Africa,' Alf continued. 'Caesar got as far as Brentford, and the story goes that Homer was born there. Who brought this coin to Southall?' The night was still, the land was preparing for frost. The whole of Middlesex was in black-out. Danny felt the immensity of the night and the past fall upon him. By daylight, he had heard enough. He came home.

Rent was £1 6s 2d per week. The house had electricity, gas, and running water. Empty cocoa tins were arranged on the kitchen windowsill. At the end of each working day, Dolly and her sister Irene filled them with small change. Emily-Elsie emptied them once a week. Every gas bill was kept, every tap washer filed in brown envelopes. Dolly, Emily-Elsie's eldest, remembered when she and her mother had moved into Cato Street, Paddington, with a man called Daniel. Home in Cato Street had been two rooms in a Victorian tenement block called Windsor Buildings. It was the kind of dwelling that turned up-and-coming areas into slums. By contrast, number 29 was a modern house planted on a leafy boulevard. The elms never achieved the desired leafiness but the thought was there. The house woke up to the smell of bread and Dolly left for her nine o'clock shift at Lyons. She took the 607 to Shepherd's Bush and the 'Tuppenny Tube' from Shepherd's Bush to Tottenham Court Road. From Tottenham Court Road, she walked to Lyons Corner House in Piccadilly. She was a Nippy, but she had been trained in silver service at the Cumberland Hotel. When the call-up came for women to work in factories, she refused. The penalty for single women refusing war work was severe. She was sent to Holloway Prison. Five days later she was released to an empty street in north London, and quickly made her way home. Unlike her sisters, Dolly had no friends or lovers.

FOOD Is a Munition of War. Don't Waste It. This was the legend printed on the Lyons menu. Some evenings, Danny would find piles of rock cakes and curly sandwiches on his bunk in the Anderson shelter. 'Don't tell anyone,' Dolly would say. 'It's our secret.' Then she gave him a shilling to swear at their mother. 'A fine fellow you are!' was Emily-Elsie's retort.

On a March morning in 1940, Danny came home. On opening the door, he couldn't hear Emily-Elsie and Dolly arguing. Mother and daughter were like birds in flight, colliding and gliding, hawking and chirruping, cooing at and chiding each other. They were two sparks alighting on combustible material. They were smooth as silk woven by lovers who cannot part.

Chapter Four

'IT'LL BE DRUGS NEXT.'

Nights were long, and I lay encased in a wood-panelled cabin listening to the rain as it hammered the hull. *Adam Bonny* was nosediving into the canal. The dust and ashes were getting the better of me. The sofa was seeping soot. When the rain paused I stocked up on provisions. Negotiating the rope bridges and lonely neighbours calling for company, I made night-time forays through Shackleton Estate to Auntie's Grocery Stores. Hooded boys in dim doorways like monks in dark cloisters scattered as I crept through the concrete walkways. I was hoping to bump into some local wildlife but it always seemed to be disappearing round a corner or fleeing up a stairwell into a low-rise block. I found Auntie. She had a twinkle in her eye – and a seductive 'Hello, dearie' – and she did special deals – three for the price of two – on Bulgarian wine.

I tore myself away from her conspiratorial smile, and the nodding turbaned heads she gathered around her, and back on the boat I set my cut-price wine to simmer with cloves, cinnamon and cider. Mug and book in hand, I curled round the stove, baking in its glow. The Gypsy had told me that my card was the Hermit, and I believed her. She showed him to me. 'He carries a lantern because he seeks out the truth in dark places.' In that darkness, I could not see how it could be found elsewhere. Boat-dwellers tend to be solitary creatures, and, for the duration of that winter, so was I.

'It'll be drugs next,' the officer said grimly. In the progression of a classic addiction, the addict ends his or her using days strung out on heroin with a syringe hanging out of his or her arm; ideally in a public toilet because he or she is living on the streets. This is the classic model. For me, it started with a bag of glue, which was the best euphoric high I ever reached (until, thirty years later, I smoked heroin). But even at the age of twelve, I knew that if I carried on with the total bliss that glue brought me, I would not be able to stop and I would end up like my uncle James, strung out on heroin with a syringe hanging out of my arm. Discipline, instilled from my mother, father and great-aunt Dolly, was my best friend. They knew the imperative of earning a living. Money was the drug that turned them on. I grew up with heroin as the rather annoying and embarrassing member of the family who let us all down. So at the age of twelve, I made the important decision not to inject heroin. Then I sat it out. Until I was fourteen, I ate boiled sweets and read thrillers. I went to school but I avoided speaking to the other girls. I was waiting till I was old enough to have a drink.

Just before Christmas 2007 I was sacked from my job at HMP Chelmsford for trafficking in books and biscuits. Besides bringing in Jaffa Cakes and Raymond Murphy's *English Grammar in Use*, I had allowed a prisoner to get close to me. No one else could (unless they had some serious amounts of drugs on them) but Freddie found a way. He was a coke-head and I liked his energy. Freddie named a star after me. His mother sent a picture of it addressed to me at the prison. The picture was intercepted by the security department. Two prison officers escorted me from the establishment.

I came home to a cold, dark boat.

'The steel hull lowers the temperature,' *Evening Star* leered. I scowled at him, convinced that he kept himself warm seeing me suffer. In fact, he collected wooden pallets from industrial estates and built towering pyres in his garden. From Orchard Street, I could hear the splutters and sparks of leftover fireworks from Divali. I refused his offer of a swig from his flask and fetched the wheelbarrow. Before I could retreat into *Adam Bonny* I had to fetch coal from Barney's weekly delivery. I fetched the wonky wheelbarrow and trundled down to the end of the dock under the bridge where the coal was stored. I heaved my tonnage of fuel back aboard and huffed and puffed at the stove until I made fire. I fed the yawning, stretching cats and wanted a drink. I had been invited to Christmas drinks aboard *Bob-A-Buoy*. I went. *Evening Star* was by now sporting a Santa hat. I made my excuses and left. I felt empty. I had been stripped of my job and my identity as a responsible member of society. My sense of myself as a woman ('Because you're worth it!' Because I wasn't) had drained with more efficiency than the bath water down the plughole into the canal. I have never understood female conventions – such as, for instance, wanting to get married and have children, or the one of talking faster and more freely when nonplussed. One thing I did agree with: applying lipstick and mascara is as good as a pep-talk. I told myself I looked good ('mature, confident, Latin in origin!'), and thus the world was full of possibilities as I climbed up the gangway, crossed the rope bridge and clanged the gate of the dock behind me.

I left my sinking boat behind me but I could not leave the sinking feeling in my stomach.

'Let's go to the Harvester,' said Pete. The Harvester was a mile from old Southall in even older Norwood Green. It had a rural feel and a slow-blinking landlord. The current draw at the Harvester was Noah. He was selling DVDs at a cut-down rate. I could see that Pete had his mind set on battening down my boat's hatches with a DVD box set, hopefully with me still on board. Noah, Pete told me, was a Romany Traveller ('a Diddycoy or do-as-you-likey unless you're PC, and we don't have time for that round here'). Much to everyone's derision, Noah claimed to be a bare-knuckle boxer. 'We all know, right, that it's Noah's brother, Duane, who is the bare-knuckle boxer,' laughed Pete. Noah was better known for having slashed open a drug dealer's stomach with a Stanley knife. The dealer had sold him some dodgy gear.

It was closing time but betting shops do not shut their doors when there is business to be done. The gambling addicts were still standing outside Ladbrokes on Orchard Street, still hedging their bets and counting their losses. Southall caters to all tastes. 'You can get anything here,' was Pete's favourite refrain. On this grimy Christmas night, desperate men stood in doorways begging for a pound. Pete was magnanimous in doling out spare change. As he did so, he told me about the dodgy businessmen in the Gurdwara Temple famed for its golden dome.

'It's the largest Sikh temple outside India,' he boasted, as he sauntered past it. In the eerie green light diffused by gold, he reminded me of a Dantesque tourist guide. On these narrow, terraced streets packed with Hindu families that came here in the 1950s, I saw their sons and grandsons, the Beemer Boys, sitting in parked cars.

'Yeah, the Beemer boys,' Pete chuckled. 'Paz, Jaz or Chaz for Pazwinder, Jazwinder or Chazwinder. Winder means worker, like Patel or Singh. You can always tell the working-class Indians. These boys are spoilt; in their mid to late thirties. Parents well off, own land in India the size of Cornwall. Managed to escape arranged marriages; will hold off till early forties and then they get an eighteen-year-old. That's why they have honour killings. These girls realise when they come here they don't have to put up with it. Then they get "run over" and shit.'

His invisible speech marks stopped me dead. But in Southall you just keep going. Even so, I was stumbling over paving slabs to keep up with him.

'These boys sell coke but they can't smoke or swear in their homes so they sit in their cars with young white girls (Indian skanks are lower than shit – they get rubbish thrown at them). You can tell how well they're doing by their licence plates. If they're doing really well it'll be a 2008 7 series, always the same – sports edition, black-tinted windows. Black dealers drive black VW Golfs, the sports edition.'

'*Teri Ma dhi!*' one of the Boys shouted to Pete.

'He's disrespecting my mum but I don't care, he's welcome to her.'

'Pakistani!' Pete shouted back, both men laughing at the trade of insults. 'Yeah. Pakistani – the lowest form of life.'

As we promenaded past them, the Beemer Boys stared at me with the effrontery that white English men, as a rule, do not possess.

'Only Italians stare at women like that,' I said.

'They think you're a prostitute,' Pete explained.

Later, it would be revealed to me why.

Chapter Five

THE GYPSIES IN THE WOOD

The Register of Common Graves states that there are eight people in the burial plot by the south wall at Hortus Cemetery – a wall so long and featureless that by the time I reached the end of it and the pub was in sight I was dragging my feet behind me, overcome by sheer monotony. My great-grandmother Emily-Elsie, mother of Dolly and Danny and my grandmother Lilian, was the fourth body to be buried on 16 March 1948. It cost £2 7s to bury her.

My mother remembered sleeping three in a bed with Dolly and Emily-Elsie. Her head lay between their calloused feet.

The last bodies interred were baby twins on 21 May. Their family could not afford a 'purchase' grave either. When I contemplate the space that holds my great-grandmother's remains, I see a stretch of grisly lawn and a concrete barrier, nothing to mark her space. Emily-Elsie is everywhere and nowhere. On paper, she occupies a pauper's grave or what is called today a 'common' grave. The new words are designed to take the sting out of the stigma. In effect, they commit a fraud. In removing the charge, they gloss over the reality of the impoverished plenty. Shame comes free, after all. It's part of the package.

I asked Pete if he knew a man called Spider, a former associate of Great-uncle Danny. The last time I had seen Spider
had been at a party at 29 Woodlands Road. Spider was a
young man, one of many who danced attendance on my
great-uncle Danny. Usually my great-uncle surrounded
himself with young Asian men. Tonight it was just Spider.
He was dark, graceful and twitchy in black jeans and a silk
waistcoat. He did not speak to me out of deference to Danny.
I was Family. But his feature gold tooth lit up in a radiant
smile when he winked at me. He had eyes that fascinated me,
eyes that said, 'Come and get me. I don't give a fuck about
myself any more. I'm all yours.' These were the eyes that told
me there were no depths we could not reach together.

I was twelve years old and still waiting for my first drink. I sat
with Dolly in the kitchen of number 29, the house where she
had been happiest. She was making rounds of sandwiches
from tinned salmon, cucumber and sliced white bread. Spider
and Danny were in the garden dancing to the radio. Despite
his largeness, Danny was light on his feet. I remember his
pirouettes around the patio, and my own embarrassment at so
much unabashed, pullulating enjoyment. My great-uncle was
a fat, lonely man whose bullying and hoarding tendencies
had made him a lot of money, and in that moment, he was
happy. There was a climax to the evening. Elders at the
Gurdwara had deemed the wearing of the kirpan as purely
ceremonial. So Spider kept his in the boot of his car. But that
night, for Danny's benefit, Surdeep, known as Spider,
Danny's darling, twirled his kirpan above his head. 'That's a
big knife, Spider,' Danny enthused.

It had been thirty years since I had seen Spider, but I sensed
his presence in old Southall. I had been having disturbing

intimations of revelation creeping over me since I had discovered Emily-Elsie's grave. It was as though, from her place of
obscurity, she were trying to tell me something. As for Spider,
I felt sure that he and Pete must have crossed paths. And I
needed an ally, the upper hand, the inside track. Spider might
be the key to solving the mystery in which I was trapped.

So I asked Pete if he knew a guy called Spider.

'We've done a bit of business together,' Pete grudgingly
admitted. 'I see him around.'

Whenever I asked Pete or his friends about their acquaint-
ances they clammed up. At these times, I felt as though I
were a policewoman, eliminating suspects in a criminal
inquiry. The caginess of my new 'associates', because, in a
sense, that was what they were, was part of my incentive for
getting to know them. I wanted to crack the code.

We skirted the Shackleton Estate and crossed the canal at
Newlocks Bridge where the roads became wider, the houses
of more architectural interest.

'I've done a lot of burglaries round here,' reflected Pete.

We stopped to look up at the second-floor window of a
detached villa. It was left open on the latch and I followed
Pete's gaze as it climbed the garage wall and leapt up and
across to the window ledge.

'It was the challenge! And then the prospect of hidden
treasure . . . I just couldn't resist.' We had been drinking and
smoking skunk since early evening, and the sharpness of
January was doing an excellent job of reviving us from our
sluggishness.

'I did burglaries because the question kept nagging at me:
what is behind that door? It was hope – hope springs eternal!
– for that pot of gold.

'Plus, of course, I was too lazy to go to work.'

The Harvester pub stood in the middle of parks and allotments that had once been brick fields. Like most itinerant workers, the brickmakers of Middlesex are a forgotten part of London's cityscape. They are commemorated only in the names of pubs, like the Brickmakers' and Bricklayers' Arms. The city grew from the mud that these men, women and children worked. Their story took me back to the origins of my own forebears, their urbanisation and my fantasies of a pastoral idyll that often dematerialised into *nostalgie de la boue*. It was easier down there. But Pete had not finished. 'On benefits you can smoke ten pounds of crack a day. After a burglary it'll be more like a hundred pounds of crack and hopefully no dead bodies.'

I could understand how someone could get to that place where burglary was the only option. But I knew Pete would never believe that I could be in the grip of his excitement. Even where I felt affinity there was no point expressing it.

The Harvester was busy. There was a games room as well as the usual saloon and public bars. Pete left me sitting in a corner while he took up his station at the pool table. A thin Indian girl with dark, greasy hair was feeding coins into a slot machine next to me. She was muttering to herself and shaking her bowed head like a horse reined in against its will. Noah came to sit by my side. I tried not to flinch at the sight of this massive, bald wreck of a man covered in scars and prison tattoos and with gold hoops in both ears. His dolefulness was more dismaying than his bulk, which was like muscle and gristle sliding down the chopping board into a pan of lard. He planted himself with a resounding thwack on the narrow wooden chair, and rested a holdall between tiny feet.

It was full of DVDs that he had 'ripped off from some Chinese'.

'Hello, love, I hear you're a writer,' he sighed.

'Now and again.' I was learning the lingo.

'But you won a prize,' he insisted.

In 2002 I won the Crime Writers' Gold Dagger for a book about my criminal grandfather. The prize-giving ceremony was held at a grand hall in the City of London. In my hurry to dispense with the bottle of red wine I had been drinking over dinner, I spilt it over my agent. He swiftly left the ceremony with a wine-stained shirt and misgivings about his client. The prize's sponsors were Macallans, distillers of whisky. By the end of the evening I was swigging from a bottle of oak-smoked single malt.

A kindly lady crime-writer put me in a taxi and sent me home. I missed the party. I sat in a taxi, on my own, brandishing my bottle and a dagger. At least I knew what to do with the bottle.

'Do you know anything about Romany culture?' Noah asked.

During Diversity Awareness Week, the men in Chelmsford Prison had shared their views of the Travelling community:

'They'll do you a dodgy driveway and you'll never see them again.'

'Fresh people, fresh money.'

'You've got to keep on the move,' a Traveller told me, 'because people get used to what's happening if you stay in one place for too long.'

'There's good and bad in every community,' pre-empted Noah. 'I'm a lump now, but I was tiny as a child.' He looked straight at me. 'You wouldn't think it, would you?' inviting me to scrutinise the length and breadth of him. 'I was born in

Tentelow Woods – that's up the canal towards Bulls Bridge. My family are Travellers on both sides – the Temples, the Hibbses, the Scamps and the Loveridges – we're all related. By the time I was born' – he looked me in the eye again – '1973,' and I hid my consternation, 'they had all moved on to land in the wood. I was born in a caravan.

'One day, when I was seven years old, I was coming home from school and a local tough nut picked a fight with me. "Dirty Gyppo", he called me. The closer I got to home, the more I was crying.'

Pete nudged his friend at the pool table as they both took a break to eavesdrop on Noah's story. Once they got the gist of it, they resumed positions and left me to listen.

'Crying isn't the done thing in Romany families. I went back to our site and my dad took one look at me and ripped the fence up and got a pole. He snapped it in two. "Go and do him," he said. "If you come back crying again, I'll hit you with it," and so it began. I went back to that boy and all I'll say is he'll never forget me.

'After that, a big war started on Newlocks and Shackleton. Pete remembers, don't you, mate?'

'Sure, sure,' Pete nodded. The Indian girl had migrated from the slots to the pool table and was plucking at Pete's jacket pocket. 'Give us a pound,' she bleated. Pete obliged.

I wondered at the sight of this woman drained of life and self-respect, and Pete's nonchalance that it should be so. It was almost comforting.

'After the first time, I got a liking for it and went into training. I would punch tree trunks with nothing on my hands to strengthen my wrists and knuckles, and my uncle Bill would throw softballs at me. I'd punch them away with my bare fists.'

'My first competitive fight took place at night, in a clearing in the woods. The other lad was my age: thirteen. His dad was called Hector Seaman and my uncle Bill had a bit of a feud with him. Bill had taken Hector's missus, Rosie, off him. So there was a bit of tension in the air. There were around fifty men standing round a roped-off, chalked-up ring. There were bales of straw stacked around it. All I remember is my uncle Bill and old Hector. My vision and my hearing zoned in on their faces. Everything else was just noise. They were steamed up, frothing at the mouth.'

I was attending to Noah's story but fidgety for a fix. The bell rang for closing time and I bought a final round, which seemed to be my last remaining purpose. I returned to Noah who was still telling his story – fresh people, fresh ears – both of us in the hope that something more fortifying would come our way. I placed two pints of Magner's cider on the table. In my delusion I believed that by drinking apple-flavoured alcohol I was imbibing one of my five portions of fruit and vegetables per day.

'It's doing me good,' I told myself as I sunk my poison.

Noah had trailed off into the realms of blatant fantasy but I happily joined him. Before I could polish off my Magner's, he was being asked to 'take a dive'.

'I was approached by a geezer high up in Traveller society. He was offering me a pay-off of £7,000. The fight was due to take place on Bixley Fields.'

The green meadow I could glimpse from my boat.

'Bixley Fields, so it was.'

By now my restlessness was seeking resolution and there was nary a cocaine dealer in sight. I could hardly stay still in my seat. I needed a hit.

'You should have seen Noah's sister.' Pete had finished his game, and was gathering his winnings. 'Bertie the Shed her name was. She was the most fanatical and dangerous female Chelsea supporter of her time, wasn't she, Noah?'

'Aye, so she was.' He sighed again, once more deprived of his denouement. Pete was studious in ignoring my wild-eyed gesticulations indicating my desire for cocaine.

'She was five foot four but she would take on six or seven men and cut the fuck out of them.'

'So she did,' Noah assented, fading back into his oversized bag of DVDs.

'She's a licensed black cab driver now,' sniffed Pete.

My anguish and the incongruity of Bertie the Shed being a taxi driver rushed up at me. I exploded into hysterical laughter. I laughed all the way back to my berth on a sinking boat.

The next day I woke up and I wasn't laughing. The sour taste of alcohol and vomit was clinging to the inside of my mouth. Remorse was clinging to the inside of my brain. Cravings were doing laps up and down the inside of my stomach. The cats needed feeding and the chemical toilet had reached saturation point. So had I. Worse, I kept identifying with the toilet. I slid out of bed to do my duties but fear and recriminations reclaimed me. There was nothing for it but to go back to bed where I could give my full attention to the accusations and counter-attacks that were being launched at an unknown combatant (though I suspected it was me) in my head. This siege was being conducted on my premises in my time without my permission. I was locked into a life-or-death balloon debate and could not leave my bed. Most addicts, at this stage, will reach for the smack or the benzos to calm themselves down and alleviate the withdrawal from alcohol. I was different. I butched it out because to cave in

and take a downer would mean admitting I had a 'problem'.
Discipline was still my best friend but it was killing me. The
grip of addiction is such that recovery literature describes it as
'cunning, powerful and baffling'. Or the recovering addict
will say, 'Addiction is an illness that doesn't want you to
know that you are ill.' In my case, my addiction had taken
such a hold that the stories it was telling me kept me locked
inside my head where I struggled not to hear them.

Nancy knocked on my cabin door before opening it.

'You must get a lock fitted,' she exclaimed. She was right.
I sank further into the hopelessness that slept alongside me
under the electric duvet that didn't work. Nancy was all
dolled up and wanted me to take her to Soho.

'Where is it?' she demanded.

She had been told by a male admirer that she could get a
job as a 'hostess'. Nancy had once worked in a nightclub.
'They loved to see me dance on a table,' she crowed, eyes
misting with the relish of past conquests. She wanted to
regain those giddy heights. As far as I could tell, being a hostess in Soho meant acquainting herself with men not dissimilar
to the husband for whom she felt so much distaste.

By the time I got to Southall I had had my fill of Soho;
exhausted its nightclubs and the phone box where dealers
gathered when clubs such as Gerry's and the Groucho failed
to hit the spot. A rumour had reached me that one club hostess was describing me as 'a vile and dangerous woman'.

My first drink in Soho was at the Pillars of Hercules on the
corner of Greek and Manette Streets. I had been working in
a bookshop on the Charing Cross Road for a week. It stood
next to Collet's, which, I was told, had direct links to the
Russian Communist Party. The hint of sedition and the

shabbiness of the shop front were tantalising. Inside, the earnestness continued with shelves of Marxist tracts, displays of Soviet memorabilia, accounts of working-class struggle and a department for folk music. I felt close to the source of an arcane knowledge that would persist in eluding me for many years. At the time, I thought it was to do with revolt. During my lunchbreak, I searched in vain for a secret society in the folk department or whispering anarchists in an alcove, plotting an insurgency. I was set to work on the third floor of the building next to Foyle's, where I had shoplifted many times in my youth.

The fame of Foyle's deep warrens and complex billing system signalled glory days for book-loving kleptomaniacs and professional thieves. We came from far and wide to steal forbidden fruits from hectically fecund shelves. Charing Cross Road was a place of temptation, mystery and legend. From my third-floor perch I could observe the hustle of Denmark Street, which had its own subculture of drug wholesalers and purveyors of musical instruments. On the corner with Charing Cross Road, directly opposite, was the Hellenic bookshop, run by an elderly Greek woman and her carelessly handsome son. He had a distracted air about him as he conducted errands involving parcels wrapped in string. He looked like he was engaged on urgent business, possibly connected to the anarchists I could not find in Collet's.

Here on the third floor, alone in the philosophy department, I sold romantic novels to myself. The Greek son of the overbearing mother might take me to a land of marble columns and the Aegean Sea. I might meet a studious, duffel-coated man with a vision, a purpose and a mission. In the meantime, I met a Russian émigré who turned up at the Pillars of Hercules, the French House and then the Coach and Horses. Like me, he knew no one, and we would sit quietly in a corner watching and admiring the more seasoned Soho habitués, waiting to be admitted into their circles. His name was Stefan, and, whatever the weather, he wore a rough woollen overcoat and an astrakhan hat. He was tall with swept-back fair hair, glacial eyes and Slavic cheekbones. He told me he had been a footballer once in America, but refused to expand. He made me prod his thigh to test the muscle. I was too embarrassed to refuse. I could confirm he certainly had sinewy muscles. His accent was thick and he never had any money. I would buy him a half of lager and he would smile as though bestowing a blessing upon me. Occasionally, he sold relics from his homeland. There were tears in his eyes as he handed them over for cash. A few years later, he disappeared as suddenly as he had appeared. At about the same time, it emerged that he was not Russian at all, but that he came from Clerkenwell, where he lived with his elderly father, a watchmaker. In retrospect, he was far too young to be casting such a Zhivagoesque shadow. But he was playing to a willing audience.

The Pillars of Hercules is mentioned in *A Tale of Two Cities*, and is named for holding up the arch that runs over Manette Street. In its turn, Manette Street is named after the character Dr Manette from Dickens's novel. This is the tail-in-mouth circularity of a city that chases its myth of origin. After closing time, the theme of sedition in the demi-monde took another turn. Underneath the arch of Manette Street, I spotted Danny La Rue's flamboyant pink hair and showman's cape. He lived in a penthouse above Foyle's, and was working his way down a queue of rent boys, sampling the lips of each upturned face. Eileen, the fruit and veg lady, set up her stall here every Friday morning, and would let no one manhandle her fruit. By close of business she was exhaling spirits like a dragon, enraged by lost, map-bearing tourists.

Before Southall, Soho was my home. From the bookshop, I migrated to literary agencies and left, frustrated by selling other people's voices. I thought I would find mine in Italy where I taught English to Italians and myself. In Rome, I fell in love with a priest. When that didn't work out, I came back to London, got the job opening packages at the *TLS* and finally returned to Soho. I felt more at ease on the *Literary Review*, a magazine that took shape in a tottering Georgian house sprung tight with cases of wine, new publications (that the 'slave' unpacked – I'd paid my dues) and enthusiasts of wine and books. I was going places. I had a boyfriend who worked in publishing. I was writing travel and arts pieces for newspapers. I had two cats and a flat in Hackney. I spent my weekends in the artists' colonies of Shoreditch and Dalston. I blagged my way round the Caribbean on a press card staying at the Hilton Spa and commissioning a catamaran to take me to cloud forests and to swim with turtles. Back in Soho, I spent most nights in the *Literary Review*'s drinking club where I assumed that everyone shared my conviction that we were acting parts written by Evelyn Waugh, though in a rather tired TV adaptation. While my career was flourishing, I contracted bulimia, was prescribed with antidepressants and on top of these, I was drinking champagne, smoking cannabis and snorting cocaine. Soho never closes its doors. I drank in the Coach, the French, the Dive, the Colony, Troy's and Bradley's (more Fitzrovia than Soho), Black's, White's, Brown's, and a funny little basement club where elderly Spaniards sat on barrels playing cards. I was drawn to lowlife, to that gleam in the eyes that signals a lack of care.

I wasn't alone. In the French House I once met a writer known for his biographies of famous artists. He was in his cups and insistent on buying rounds of Ricard. His circle included a trio of French sailors in full stripy-shirted regalia and a transvestite clarinettist. 'Only in the French House could this happen,' was how I bought into it. I thought my career in drinking would get me somewhere. But then he turned. The change in mood and aspect was very sudden, and started in his eyes, which narrowed, and then reached his mouth, which snarled. As for me, I grew tired of Bohemia's mythologies. I turned round and bit the hand that fed me.

So January, like the early morning commuters, passed me by, and February arrived. I was drowning my sorrows to ease the noise between my ears. After each bout, I made myself wallow in the misery I had caused myself without hope of relief. I waited three days (just as, as an adolescent, I had waited two years for my first drink), before I would allow myself another trip to the Brickmakers' or the Harvester. My world had shrunk to the three points of a triangle: two pubs and a boat. I spent three days out of every week hiding on the boat, sweating and crying and experiencing waves of foreboding. I waited three days because I had once read in a magazine that this is how long it takes the liver to detox from binge-drinking. This is how suggestible I was. Once the three days were over, I could start again. In a way, not using drugs was more painful than using them because I couldn't say I had a problem but I knew I had madness in me. The problem was I didn't know what it was called.

Chapter Six

GUNS OF BRIXTON

It was 1979 and I was fourteen. I lived with my mother and great-aunt Dolly in a block of flats on Brixton Hill. Mould grew like seaweed on the walls. Every year, my mother would paint to hide the mould, but back it came. As the years passed, my mother's resolve crumbled and her joie de vivre diminished. My graceful, witty mother, who had flown around the world in the smartest of uniforms on the fastest of jumbo jets, had come to land in a late-twentieth-century block similar to the first home of her childhood. At times, her mood lifted, and I was granted access to a gaiety that was exhilarating – crêpes Suzettes, as opposed to mere pancakes, on Shrove Tuesday, truffles from Harrods for an after-dinner treat, Mozart on the radio.

'If there is a heaven, this is it.'

But her conscientiousness as a mother lay heavily on her. Meals had to be nutritionally balanced, and the responsibility to provide day after day for year after year was a terrible strain, leaving no room for the delights of a subtle palate. Besides, I was an ungrateful daughter, unappreciative of her efforts, preferring my own company to hers. My mother ached with grief and seclusion. There was no one to speak

French with her, or to delight in the ingenuity of the *Times* crossword. I was absorbed in a different kind of puzzle – how to hide from her.

Tom Jones, a Welsh taxi driver, lived on the ground floor. His son Mick was in a band called The Clash. His wife Gwen enjoyed mail-order shopping from Freeman's catalogue. If it hadn't been for her nylon trouser suits, Gwen could have passed for Siouxsie Sioux. Her dyed purple helmet of hair had a streak of white. Her eyes were caked with sky-blue paste, her lashes were spikes, and her lipstick was orange, lined with crimson. She was permanently poised between fury and laughter. Every day after school she would look out for me climbing the stairs to our second-floor flat. She would invite me in to show me her catalogue. Her kitchen, which had not been disturbed since the 1950s, smelt of sherry, roast meat, and cabbage. Its Formica tops were preserved in a layer of dust and grime. We drank tea infused with Bristol Cream, and perused the pages of her catalogue. When Mick came to visit, Gwen opened the door to reveal two spidery young men back-combing their Mohicans in the hall mirror. They were playing a gig that night in Brixton. I stood in the door-way waiting for them to notice my mini-kilt, monkey boots and fishnets. My carefully assembled outfit was fresh from the pages of Freeman's, and I was paying Gwen 50 pence per week for kitting me out. I failed to make an impression. As Gwen closed the door behind me, I realised something I could not put my finger on had passed me by.

'Guns of Brixton' was released that year – the same year that Blair Peach was killed down the road from the Hambrough Tavern in Southall. Great-uncle Danny was in the saloon bar when it all kicked off.

He'd done well for himself. It was rumoured he had made his fortune from selling Rubik's Cube – a rumour he himself started. He owned shops on The Broadway – shops that sold everything cheaper than you could believe. So it was within the bounds of possibility that as the sole purveyor of Rubik's Cube in Southall, he had hit the million mark. Something that was kept closer to his chest was that he knew some baggage handlers at Heathrow Airport. He also ran the doors of all the nightclubs on a five-mile radius of the M4. The Target, the Seagull and Byron's were the jewels in his crown. He left it to his mates in the Hambrough to infer from this that he was providing a service, keeping young people safe in clubs notorious for violence.

'Spider,' he said tonight from his perch in the saloon. 'I'm not a happy man.'

Spider wiped the perspiration from his brow, and looked around him. He had just plugged the jukebox with shrapnel to drown out the fug of voices in the bar, the noise of demonstrations in the street and the remonstrations circulating in his head. A visit to the toilet for a refuel had not been helpful.

'Why's that, Danny?' he sniffed.

Danny placed a piece of A4 paper torn from an exercise book into Spider's hand. Spider held it up, clenched between two fists. A spider's web tattooed in blue ink decorated both sets of knuckles. Written in biro on the piece of paper were two columns. One column listed the dates of weekends and the other cash received. Spider scanned the columns. There was an awkward silence.

'I think you know why I'm unhappy, Spider,' said Danny.

Spider was a Holy Smoke, the first Punjabi gang in England. The Holy Smokes came from the Gurdwara Temple in old Southall. Their territorial rivals were the Tooty Nungs, younger Punjabis who came from the temples in new South-all. Between them, the Holy Smokes and Tooty Nungs ran Southall. Danny occupied the ground between them. He knew that his boys, who were recruited from the whites-only working men's club, could take Spider for unpaid debts from dealing at his nightclubs. Spider knew that a splinter group from the Holy Smokes could take Danny to save the £2,000 Danny claimed Spider owed him. But Spider liked to keep the big man happy, and Danny liked this Indian lad.

'You know why I'm unhappy, Spider,' Danny repeated. After all, business was business.

'I don't. I don't know,' Spider responded, biding for time.

'You've walked past me sitting here at the bar three times. You've ignored me, and you know you owe me money.' Danny raised his voice in response to the sound of sirens and crowds gathering on the pavement outside.

Spider seized the moment. 'There's skinheads outside, Danny.' He gestured towards the bay window jutting on to The Broadway. 'They're cutting Sikhs' hair and shit, and Sikhs are doing shit back.'

One of Spider's many gods must have been on his side that night. Danny had to concede that something was up in Southall. Leaders of the National Front were holding a meet-ing at the Town Hall. Southall's Punjabi residents were objecting. Spider was itching to do something about it. He was more used to fighting Tooty Nungs over who had the best religion and who had the right to sell *atta*. (*Atta* is the Punjabi word for the fine white flour that is kneaded with water to make chapattis.) These were whites from east London – twenty miles away – that were on his patch.

'They're disrespecting us, Danny,' which was the perfect excuse to defer business. He knew he could not pay the debt.

The demand was still there: 'There's five hundred people in each club,' Danny reasoned with the slow, sure logic that made Spider fidget with impatience (He knew! He knew!). 'You should be selling at least one hit each to a third of them.' Of course he should, but it wasn't demand that was Spider's problem, it was supply. In the last four weeks, two of his dealers had been busted, and with them gone, he was 2,000 billies down. Both men knew that these misfortunes did not figure in Danny's logic: Spider owed Danny £2,000.

Danny, Dolly's fly-away boy, had hardened. Thirty years previously, when the Tony Brothers' ice-cream parlour was famed throughout Southall, he had watched the hearse carrying his dear old mum's body, consoled by spearmint lollies supplied by the Tonys, bought by Dolly. Maybe she had thought that, like ice, grief would melt in the mouth. Now he rose like a mountain from his stool in the Hambrough. His eyes were slits that took the narrow view. Danny's treasures were just for him. He liked people to be smaller than him. But he liked young men; he liked their energy. He liked Spider.

On the night of the 1979 Southall riots, more than forty people, including twenty-one policemen, were injured, three hundred youths were arrested, and Blair Peach, an anti-racism activist, was beaten to death on a side road behind the Town Hall. It was the most violent rioting in London's history, according to a statement from the police. As such, there was no question of crowd control, claimed a witness, it was a case of 'the boot going in'.

Vague suspicions were playing on Danny's mind, and he could not quell them. His oversized stomach lurched with fear and his heart strained with intimations of betrayal. He experienced a rare awakening as his reasoning stilled, silence descended and clarity dawned. In that moment, he knew that Spider had loyalties that far outreached his orbit, and that he would act on them come what may. He shook his head before the thought could occur that Southall had grown too big for him.

On Christmas Day that year, my mother, my great-aunt Dolly and I watched an episode of *Porridge*. A character called Grouty triggered memories of that house in Woodlands Road, and the working men's club round the corner from it. I remembered Great-uncle Danny presiding over Bingo and drinks for everybody. I realised that Great-uncle Danny would not be out of place in *Porridge*. But when I pointed this out there was a loaded silence. My mother made no comment. Instead she aired an old grievance. She told me about the time he had thrown a dart at her. She was seven years old. She still had the scar above her eyebrow where Danny's dart had missed her eye. He had been aiming for the dartboard, he explained.

In the spring of 1980, a stash of guns was found in the shed in the garden of 29 Woodlands Road. Danny was imprisoned in HMP Wormwood Scrubs on charges of possession of firearms. The house that held so many memories was also the repository of Spider's secrets. Even though he took the rap, Danny refused to see the betrayal. He came home defeated but he could not afford to comprehend it. That same spring I was fifteen years old and had been developing a tolerance for Pernod & Black for just over a year. The sugar high on its own was enough to convince me that I was in love with a skinhead called Glen. We held hands over the bar table of a south London pub for two weeks.

After three weeks, Glen 'chucked' me. I was so high on sugar and love I did not even realise that it was over. This was handy for Glen as a week or so later he needed me to provide an alibi. There had been a murder late one night on Clapham Common. Glen asked me to testify to the police that I had been with him on the night of the murder. I agreed and listened to what he told me I was to tell the police. The facts were that I had not been with Glen the night of the murder and that I did not know where Glen had been on the night in question. The facts never came into it. Glen and I held hands all the way to the police station.

One morning in March, from my cabin porthole, I watched goldfinches teasing out the fluff from hawthorn bushes. That evening – port side of my barge, I heard a splash and a scream followed by crazed gurgling. It was Nancy. She had fallen into the canal, and she was laughing.

'Why don't you leave the boat?' she asked me.

I recruited Nancy as the Ratty to my Mole. We boarded the train to Paddington and took a bus to Portobello Road. Outside the Fat Badger pub we were joined by a familiar figure. I was beginning to find significance in chance encounters. This man was tall and adroitly shabby. He had a pint in his hand and he was smiling and greeting passers-by. A boy from the fishmonger's on Golborne Road called out his name. 'Mick' waved back graciously. Then I realised who it was, and time came flooding back to me: a time before sinking boats, demon dock owners and retired burglars. Mick Jones took me back to my emergence into adolescence and a riot-torn urban sprawl. I could not wait to get back to my refuge on a sinking boat. Still drenched in wine-soaked memories, I reached Southall Station. I saw the same view Great-uncle Danny had seen. The landmarks against a watery-blue sky were wreathed in pale grey. The railway tracks on course to Maidenhead and beyond were telling the same story. Now it was duplicated in Punjabi script.

Too much booze and twilight made Nancy similarly nostalgic.

'My husband is an Englishman,' she said. 'I was seventeen when we met.'

'What does he do?'

'He raises funds for charities in Africa.'

'How did you meet him?'

'I met him in a nightclub.'

'Where is he now?'

'Saudi Arabia.'

'Why aren't you with him?' I wondered aloud.

'I don't like him,' she smiled.

Tempest still sits in the basin of the dock where hedgerows turn into jungle, and lights from the factory spark all night. Nancy received a monthly allowance from her husband.

'Is your family still in Ghana?' I asked.

'My mother is, but my father died a long time ago,' she explained. 'All I remember is a big man in a white suit, always laughing. He used to come to our compound with friends, and pass out drunk after partying. He was very rich. My mother and my aunt would go through his pockets for money.'

'How did he die?' I asked.

'He was shot.'

I looked startled.

'One of his wives hired a hit man to shoot him.'

We walked in silence along Orchard Street. Southall-wallahs call this *prana* Southall, which means it's too old and run-down for Punjabis, but, because of this, you can still get good deals. Orchard Street is home to Somalis and since they like to do business on street corners, it's lively. This liveliness

– dark-skinned men gathering outside internet cafés on ill-lit pavements – is alien to the few remaining, highly suspicious white residents.

'Do you think Somali pirates listen to the Shipping Forecast?' I asked Pete. He raised an eyebrow and potted the pink he'd been after.

It's always dark in old Southall. Orchard Street is a narrow, Victorian high street, resistant to the demands of modern traffic. Horns hoot. Car stereos blare out Bollywood numbers. Hopper buses and buses proper lurch from stop to stop, abused by Beemers and Peugeots. The Tudor-beamed Manor House on the Green with its gables and bay windows dates back to 1587. The stocks stood at the corner of its grounds – a space now occupied by the Himalaya Palace where Miss Pooja, Apache Indian and Charanjeet Channi are the home-grown talent at the Music Night: *Punjabi By Nature*. The Three Horseshoes . . . there was a time when, on Wednes-days, all roads led to Southall, when all the medley of the horse market was in full swing. It was the recruiting sergeant's happy hour and the Three Horseshoes his headquarters. Admirers would throng to his smart red uniform and his perch at the bar, buying the drinks. 'They came, they saw, and they were conquered.' A number of these recruits joined the 4th Dragoons, afterwards to be sent to the Crimea. This week, the Three Horseshoes had Desmond on Friday from eight till two and Mikey on Saturday for an Irish party. Next to them, a window display lit up the early evening gloom with glass images of Ganesha, Laxmi and many more. Up to eighty per cent off and then there's peri peri chicken at the Lick'n Chick'n & Pizza shop.

Nancy recommended the peri peri — 'It's better than Nando's' — and in the next breath she scorned Mona Lisa Hair and Beauty's special offer on Touch Me! whitening cream. However, she confided with a giggle, she did use their exclusive concoction of 'soft and beautiful brown henna' to streak her extensions. I looked again — her glossy locks of hair in alternating colours were attached to her scalp with lead pins. Nancy certainly put the effort in, but it was her nonchalance that was appealing. She also had an intelligence that animated her face more than make-up could. 'Come in here.' She edged me into the narrow doorway of a bazaar. 'These places are so weird,' and so I followed her.

The bazaar was like a rabbit warren burrowing through the ground floor and basement of a shabby Victorian mansion block. Each stall was blasting its own Eastern prayer or Bollywood musical. The air was thick with incense and darting brown eyes. On their ramshackle stalls, we found more special offers: dates from the Kingdom of Saudi Arabia, orange-flavoured instant drink, no-guarantee scramble-channel remote control, 'fast transfer you can trust'. Deep in the bowels of the bazaar were the insignia of a revived religion, pamphlets in Arabic script, and dusty knitted caps worn by Islamo-chavs and the real deal, the men with sun-blanched eyes and sand-blown faces.

We stopped at the corner of Orchard Street.

'I used to come here when I was a little girl,' I told Nancy. 'There was a working men's club here, and my great-uncle was the Bingo caller.'

Danny lording it over the blue-rinsed ladies, getting the drinks in, the local boy done good.

'The club was whites only, and closed down in the '80s.'

Generally speaking, Nancy was a good listener. It was not just her studied politeness, it was her natural curiosity that made her stop to listen. But for reasons with which I totally sympathised, Nancy was for the time being uninterested in local history or race relations.

'They're smoking khat,' she said, and sashayed down the road like a black swan trailing gauzy fabric. I followed her progress towards a cluster of shifty-eyed men sitting on packing cases outside an electronics retail outlet. We were across the road from a brand new mosque and a few doors down from my memories of Danny's Bingo nights. Car horns competed with the call to prayer. Turbaned drivers called out their appreciation of Nancy. But she was not the only beautiful black girl in Southall. A Somali in full hijab regalia sauntered past us. As she did so, I felt Nancy stiffen with resentment. She turned her back on the girl and flashed her teeth at the men. I, too, was struck by the opulence of the features emerging from the veil. Her painted lips were like bruised blackcurrants, and her extravagantly made-up eyes were round and liquid with pleasure. Her veil was a statement. 'You don't need to see the rest. You know I'm beautiful.'

Somali women are renowned for their good looks, and 'underneath those veils, they like attention', Pete averred.

Reputation is everything in Southall, and Somali men consider women as part of their territory – just like drugs, something else that makes the eyes liquid with pleasure.

Gabriel, Pete's best mate, with a scar down the side of his face, gave this warning to Southall's newcomers. 'Stay away from their girls. Sammies use knives first and ask questions later.' You only had to look at the red crescent on his cheek to know that this was a warning backed up with painfully acquired evidence. It usually earned him a drink – 'Foster's, please, mate' – a free game of pool and a pat on the shoulder.

I joined Nancy and a friendly electronics merchant from the Middle East in the store-room of his shop. The walls were shelved with wide-screen plasma TVs and row upon row of crates layered with blue plastic bags. The bags contained bouquets of khat, £3 a bag. Nancy ran through the procedure.

'You tear the leaves off a few at a time, chew, then spit them out. Then you chew on Wrigley's for a while. Then you start again.'

A few hours later, the evening rush hour had quietened down and we were sitting with the men on packing cases outside the electronics shop, chewing as contentedly as cows in a meadow. The late-night grocers' and curry houses of old Southall were like Christmas fairy lights in the darkness. Coming round the same corner we had just come from, although I couldn't be quite sure of when that was, I saw a man I could not place.

'This stuff is hypnotising,' I said to Nancy.

'It's a stimulant,' she replied.

'It's both,' our salesman smiled.

It was Spider. The name of the man hesitating on the corner of Orchard Street came to me like the gold rush of his grin at Nancy. But then he spotted my puzzled gaze give way to recognition. As did she, and she turned away, demure and unconcerned. Just as I realised who I had seen, he turned his back on us. Before I could call out his name, he had retraced his steps up Orchard Street, going deeper into old Southall.

'Do you know that man?' I asked Nancy.
'What man?' And there was that smile again.

Nocturnal Southall: Somali men sit in their cars all night, chewing. The women drive up to suppliers, buy it, and take it home, where they sit all night in their living rooms, chewing. I left the pleasure-eaters on their packing cases chewing methodically on Wrigley's and khat. The streets of Southall are strewn with leaves, but they are not from trees that grow in London. High on khat, and looking for answers, I followed Spider into old Southall.

Danny crossed a bridge across a canal. There was a man who sold roasted chestnuts. It was warm standing shivering in front of his charcoal fire . . . waiting for punters to take pity. He bided his time staring at a distant tin can – the gasometer – on the horizon. He wished he could find the opener.

Chapter Seven

GARDEN OF EDEN

'I had it all, Nancy.'

'What do you mean?'

'I had prospects.'

'What happened?'

'I threw it away.'

'Why?'

'It wasn't enough.'

The dock was entered through a padlocked gate. On one side was a long, bumpy towpath. On the other side, at every few feet, the concrete bank was studded with an iron ring, to which each barge owner tied the stern of their craft. The boats lay packed together like proverbial sardines, with strips of garden dictated by the length of each narrowboat, Dutch barge or tug. Each garden reflected the owner's character. Mine had unmown lawn and unmanicured hedgerows and the shade of rowan trees. At the end of the daisy chain, *Tempest* luxuriated in the pool that circled the factory. Behind the hedge and knots of tree, Bixley Fields spread into a waste-land of derelict caravans and car-repair workshops. Once they had been paint shops, forges, beer shops and stores for the brickmakers who settled here.

Nancy and I were preparing for a punt up the canal. Smoke was billowing from *Tempest*'s chimney like steam from a pudding. Roses were painted round her portholes in brilliant curlicues of scarlet and green. *Bob-A-Buoy* was on standby. He had been recruited to untie the rope bridges that crossed the dock.

My ancestral voices were calling me. I kept digging deeper into their history and discovering their sojourn further down the canal in the Basin. On days like this when Nancy and I took *Tempest* out (*Adam Bonny* had no engine, I had discovered), I found another source of inspiration.

Tempest was so trim she needed little or no steering, just a steady hand at the tiller and a mindful eye on approaching traffic. Once we had turned left out of the dock we were on a straight stretch to Three Bridges, Brunel's masterpiece of engineering. Road, rail and canal intersect each other and fields in between keep the peace. Nancy kept the pace slow and the motor was gently buzzing in the still, warm air.

'Do you know,' I told her, 'there was a Tudor princess imprisoned near here for marrying a commoner?'

'Who was that?'

'Lady Mary Grey. She was a hunchbacked midget and the youngest sister of Lady Jane Grey, Queen of England for nine days.'

I was drawing blanks with Nancy, but she was a polite and open-hearted girl who was generous with her friendship and attention.

'I often think of Lady Mary in her attic cell, and how patient she must have been. When you spend that much time alone,' of course I was talking about myself, 'you gain the vision of a solitary.' (Or go mad.)

'Did she have visions?'

'I like to think so. The clues are there. The books she read. The company she kept at Court. She lived life on the edges of society. She went against the wishes of the Queen and married a commoner – who was also the tallest man in court. He was six foot eight. Imagine! She was a midget!'

'Did love make them blind? Did people laugh at them?'

'The Spanish Ambassador said she was the ugliest woman at Court.'

'That's not nice.' Nancy had a straightforward, childlike directness that made me love her.

'Her favourite dress was in yellow and black stripes. So she would have looked like a –'

'Bumblebee.' Nancy smiled indulgently.

'She was a fairy princess!'

We were passing open fields on one side and temporary moorings of tangled boats on the other. There were no signs of life and the peacefulness was almost oppressive. I have always had a vague fear that life is happening elsewhere. In the depths of Southall, the rest of London seemed very remote. But it was here that I found some kindred spirits. Lady Mary Grey was one of them. She was a footnote in history, but she had special significance.

'I feel she's still here,' I told Nancy.

'Yes, buzzing like a bee.'

I drew comfort from the thought of Lady Mary watching the forests of Southall and Norwood Green grow into brick fields and then into streets. She supervised Brunel's navigation of the canal, the creation of the dock, and the world's largest margarine factory. She watched the building of Gillette Corner and saw German bombers using it as a navigation guide. She saw the race riots and the murder of Blair Peach, the Holy Smokes and the Tooty Nungs. I envisioned

Mary returning to a series of curious colour plates: one showed a barge on the Grand Union Canal. The other showed the Brickmakers' Arms, once a mere beer shop. On show in the toilet, where Pete keeps his stash, is a five-metre roll of tin foil that resembles a light sabre from *Star Wars*. Martel bottles, plastic bottles, spoons, one-ml hypodermics, lighters, wrappers, Jif squeezy lemons and Vitamin C packets. Pete is hyper-vigilant tonight because he is in possession of various quantities of heroin, crack cocaine, amphetamine, dexamphetamine and skunk, enough to get him some 'intent' charges at the very least. No wonder his eyes are darting.

It was a lemon-yellow spring day ripening into green. Even the water gleamed turquoise with a large, indigo cave system beckoning beneath the prow as we approached Three Bridges lock. The canal broadened here, making room for an island. With its whitewashed stone and black paint, it offered a stunning contrast to the blue-rinsed water. I was reminded with a flood of joy of the first home of my childhood. Creeks, shallows, headlands and reefs were perfect for lying in wait and staging surprise attacks. As a child I recruited other children to play at pirates – it was part of the history of the island to which our parents had come for work.

Nancy and I moored *Tempest* at the Three Bridges layby and, armed with a bottle of rosé, through an opening on the towpath we entered the Brent River Valley. A willow dangled its branches into the river's ripples merging sage with blue and violet. This part of the parkland had been left to Nature, untended and gently drifting into woods. We sat on the banks of the river, for a moment delighting in the buzz of foraging insects and the smallness of things.

Nancy told me her husband was coming back to England.

'His partner has run off with all the funds for the charity.'

Nancy's husband, who was in his seventies, took her to Singapore when she was seventeen. He left her there, she found work as a hostess in a nightclub, and he came back a year later to marry her.

'I let him kiss me on the mouth in front of the registrar.' She pouted to show me how that worked. 'But that was it. We have not had any sex since then.'

Once again I found that, when Nancy discussed her marriage, I was not sure what to say. So she continued.

'He and his partner use prostitutes.' Her brilliant eyes narrowed in disapproval.

My solution, when it arrived, was brutally simple. 'Divorce him and get a job.'

I was becoming like Pete. Nancy, like me, was embroiled in the local nightlife. She was juggling various boyfriends spectacularly well. I felt a kind of pride as though she were my mischievous daughter who had got the better of unfeeling, caddish men. As though it was all a game of one-upmanship that would never end. I saw myself along with the other habitués of Southall as Lady Mary's unhinged descendants: separate and unheeded in a settlement west of the city. Pete and his pals occupied the Brickmakers' Arms, driven by forces greater than themselves to meet their needs. This made them as ruthless as Tudor monarchs. Like Lady Mary, a pupil of Dr John Dee, I was using a kind of alchemy to change the way I felt and to govern my future. The Court revel was being played in the gutter.

Bob-A-Buoy had had his fill of scheming and reflected on it in the snugness of his book-filled boat. We drank strong brown tea from an earthenware teapot that brewed on a hotplate on the stove. He showed me pamphlets produced by the Freedom Press. They were stacked up high enough to form a tower perilously close to leaning into the stove. *Bob-A-Buoy* had once had links with a radical anarchist syndicate in Lambeth, an offshoot of the Angry Brigade. Small explosives were their stock in trade, causing happenings at media level, and not too much collateral damage.

'Our north London comrades planted a bomb in 1970 as an early protest of the women's movement,' he told me. 'We wanted to fire the imagination of the audience for Miss World.' His eyes gleamed with waywardness above a china mug that had been doing service since the 1970s. The rain was flirting with the hull.

'A spring shower to wash away the grime of winter.' It was like being in a cave under a waterfall, as *Bob-A-Buoy* gave me a potted history of Southall's working classes and its byways.

'The medieval peasant lived hard,' he started. 'He sang songs about the western wind.'

I was following my line of labourers and finding determination and defiance in their movements. I told *Bob-A-Buoy* of their whereabouts and he told me about the witch cults of the Middle Ages. His method of narration was as strangely captivating as the early societies he conjured. In the dank gloom of his boat I felt the thrill of secret knowledge. I was in the presence of a man who had memorised arcane truths because he knew no one would believe them. 'Where is the evidence for his assertions?' I could hear the *TLS* querying. But I was rapt with attention. *Bob-A-Buoy* poured another cup of Tetley's and told me about the boldness of the early witch cults; their anti-clericalism that was political in its manoeuvring.

'These weren't just people who tried to work spells,' he nodded meaningfully.

I thought of Lady Mary and her book of John Dee's abstractions.

'Your ancestors' — he was including me in the magic circle — 'had a special Nature religion . . . The Lamb, the Wolf, the Lion . . . The god of the witches could change his shape as he chose.'

I thought of Lady Mary and her six-foot-eight commoner. I thought of myself and a midnight rambler. But *Bob-A-Buoy* was getting political. This was fine by me. The peasants began to hope — around the time of the 1381 Revolt. I liked the idea of organised subversion. Abroad there were the Communes at Ypres, and the secret peasant societies spreading through Germany — I thought of my father's German grandmother on his father's side but dismissed her immediately. Unfortunately, it was becoming clear to me that most of my ancestors had bourgeois aspirations rather than revolutionary fervour. There was no allegiance to the Union of the Shoe or the Poor Conrads for them.

Meanwhile, *Bob-A-Buoy* persisted. 'Witch cults saw a revival, rather like proto-Marxist cells.'

This was stirring stuff. The sweep of history was as determined and irresistible as the streaming rain. And then, of course, there were the artists.

'Before Mr Waddington's meadow became known as Waddy's Dump, the Martin Brothers opened their studio near by, close to where the Gurdwara stands.' The Martin Brothers, sculptors of the grotesque, had a pottery kiln a hundred yards from my favourite haunt, the Brickmakers'.

Bob-A-Buoy smoothed open a map. Like a palimpsest where there had been a market garden there was now a Wimpey works. The fruit orchards that had supplied Southall market were light industry now. On one side of the dock, the only green space remaining was Hortus Cemetery, where Emily-Elsie was.

All I could see was Ophelia drifting down the canal like a blue cord leading to a socket on another page.

Before I could get to this other page, Nancy and I decided to buck against the trend. Every now and again we would forswear alcohol and men in favour of camomile tea and culture. We visited Southall Library to see the Martin Brothers' strange, grimacing pots. Gleaming artefacts in the browns and blues of bargeware were ranged on shelves in glass cabinets. 'The kiln was just next to the Brickmakers',' I marvelled once more as though the Martins' artistic endeavours were redeeming my efforts to drink myself to death in the bar next door. In the glass of the cabinet I caught Nancy sneaking a peak at her cranberry glaze and false eyelashes. I checked my own appearance. I was on my regular health drive – three successive days without alcohol – and my eyes had opened up, my hair recovered some smoothness. I have never been entirely taken up with my own attractiveness because I don't entirely believe in it. I just counted on it as being what it was. This was what Pete saw in me: a carefree confidence that meant I did not need to play the game of competing for male attention. This was only because I rarely found the prize worth having. However, I was growing increasingly dependent on the spark of sexual chemistry to make me feel alive.

One night a fire broke out – not at the pottery, but in the Martins' shop in Holborn. The brothers were rarely seen again. They left behind their pots decorated with herons, reeds and fabulous fish. Nancy and I pondered the gallery long enough to fool ourselves that art was the reason for our excursion. From the window of the gallery above the library, Orchard Street beckoned. We climbed down the stairs.

'The Aldi Arms', I called it, because it was cheap without being cheerful. We sat at a table by ourselves – it was early afternoon so Pete and his cohort were still recovering from whatever class A bender had possessed them. Nancy floated in her usual diaphanous garb and I sauntered after her as though I did not care. No one stirred. Nancy tutted. I ordered a vodka and V2O each. The other punters were too far gone to concern us, or so I thought. Nancy put the jukebox on – a Bollywood classic – and started twirling round the darkened afternoon dive bar. I tried to ignore her, especially when I saw Elvis, the elderly black man who had once been a pimp and who was rattling with withdrawals, pull up a chair. He was hoping for an impromptu lap dance. Nancy obliged. My heart sank.

I have noticed that the rising thrill of anticipation that starts in the pit of my stomach is actually looking forward not to satisfaction but to the downward heave of disappointment. Like a gambler, I am addicted to losing. It is my safety net and the rollercoaster ride that gets me there is the only dead-cert I know. This was a no-show, a non-starter.

I was looking for my smooth talker, quick to steal and full of artifice, trickery and trade. Just as the tallest man in court had charmed Lady Mary, I was waiting for Pete's sardonic gaze. Later in the year, on 12 August 1565, when the sunny glow of summer was at its height, Lady Mary Grey, the granddaughter of Charles Brandon, first Duke of Suffolk, and Mary Tudor, former Queen consort of France, married Thomas Keyes, the Sergeant Porter at Westminster Palace. It was a secret ceremony conducted in candlelight in Thomas's apartments above the Water Gate. The bride was twenty, the groom was forty-two. Their marriage lasted nine days, as did Lady Mary's sister, Lady Jane Grey, as Queen of England. But that is another story.

Chapter Eight

I FOLLOW IN GREAT-UNCLE DANNY'S FOOTSTEPS

One night I could not find Pete. 'He's on a crack binge,' said Gabriel, and 'he prefers to be alone for the duration.' I could understand this. No real addict wants to share their drugs. Quite often I would be holed up in the toilet of the Brickmakers' doing coke, ignoring the pleas of working girls banging on the door begging for a line. But tonight Spider had taken up residence in the bar. He had just made a pick-up from Elvis the dealer, so I knew he was 'holding'.

I followed him from the Brickmakers' Arms up Orchard Street at the top of which he crossed the Grand Union and passed what used to be Norwood Mills. Close by, there was once a thatched cottage that belonged to Josiah Wedgwood. Norwood Green was, and to a large extent still is, a pretty wooded district, even though beer-drinking and revelry have been carried on here since the nineteenth century. Spider was rushing to another watering hole – the Harvester pub and the allotments that lay behind it. He picked up a female accomplice in the games room. The long-haired, sad-eyed girl I had seen before was grateful to be released from her servitude at the slot machine. Other prominent citizens of Southall were playing poker. Sweet Toof was not so tickled to see Spider there to gamble, given that Spider owed him a score. But Spider waved a bull's-eye at him, and said that Sweet Toof shouldn't mind losing a score or two 'for old time's sake'. Sweet Toof never saw the bull's-eye because Spider and the girl with the long dark hair and sad eyes disappeared over the wall of the beer garden. I watched them cross the fields beyond.

'Where were you last night?' I asked Pete the following day at the Brickmakers'. It was all very well drinking myself to death, but I could not get drunk and I needed to get high.

'Oh, I was out and about, pressing the flesh, seeing to business,' he equivocated. I looked at this skinny wraith who kept a hold on me by means of magic tricks wrapped in cling film.

'Carly always seems to reappear when he's seeing someone,' Shelby, a down-and-out sex worker, had said, before coquettishly placing herself in the lap of Elvis. Shelby would periodically sweep along Orchard Street like a metal detector scouring mudbanks. Once alerted, she would click an internal switch and spring into action. I have never seen anyone's eyes light up so fast as Shelby's.

'Don't listen to Shelby,' scoffed Pete. 'She fucks her stepfather for skag.'

'Who's Carly?' I asked him.

The first time we had smoked heroin Pete had told me about the love of his life but somehow her name escaped us both. This was Pete's special talent – to plant seeds of doubt and then rake over them. He was in no hurry to remind me of his lost love who was possibly not so lost after all.

'No one you need worry about, sweetheart,' he replied. 'Have a go on this,' and he passed me a joint.

*   *   *

I could not get a grip on myself or my spivvy boyfriend, so I went back to my family tree and circled the only man I remembered from Dolly's stories: my great-grandfather. Daniel Kingham.

'Why do you spend all this time looking for dead people?' Nancy asked.

I was getting lost. The trunk twined upwards from decayed roots, out of a landscape resembling what I imagined to be the homeland of the 'bog Irish' that my great-aunt Dolly used to mock. Muddy swamps and swirling waters, stumps of old bark and thwarted rock; sturdy boots and a stout cane were required. Then, subdividing, the trunk rose and opened out with the most singular contortions, the most illogical interlacing, knots and tangles, to convey the capricious births and deaths of offspring and comings and goings of parents. Generations crossed; illicit liaisons bore hybrid fruits at the same time as their pure-bred, older siblings reproduced. All this activity caused the branches to lengthen and intermingle like snakes in the grass. As with everything else in my life, my genealogical road map was getting messy.

Nancy had come to the rescue after my calls of distress while cleaning the boat. She had come specially prepared with her black and gold extensions in rollers under a shower cap – like a glamorous Mrs Mop – and stories of solitary excursions to Ealing's nightclubs.

'Then I went to a lap-dancing club. I was the only woman there!' she said. I knew that Nancy was intrepid but I worried about her need for attention. It niggled at me though I could not locate the source of discomfort. Apart from the reflection she provided, I could see where Nancy was heading and I wanted to spare her. I resumed my search for dead people to compensate for my powerlessness over the living.

'I'm looking for the warmth of a family because my own left me out in the cold,' I wanted to tell her, 'and I can't find my way back to the warmth.' Too self-dramatising.

'Since before I can remember I have felt alone in an unkind universe.' Again, stop with the drama!

'Everyone, my father, my mother, my grandmother, teachers, uncles and aunts – they were always too busy to listen. Or there was always something else more important going on. In the end, even Dolly let me down. It was called "a catatonic state", my mother told me.' This was too long-winded and I feared my capacity for despair was lurching towards self-pity. Whatever the case, it was too late. I couldn't find the words. This was why I had to come here and confide in a burglar.

Pete had a creeper's talent for listening so it was like talking to no one. But he gave me the summing-up with which I repeatedly silenced myself.

'It's over. It's done. Move on!' And he rubbed the chalk into his cue.

Before I could have the satisfaction of moving on, I had to reach the end of him.

Chapter Nine

MAY DAY MAY DAY

Emily-Elsie Smith, my great-grandmother, was born in London in 1888. By the beginning of the twentieth century, her parents, her sisters and her aunt Cecilia had left for sunnier climes, Southend-on-Sea. Emily-Elsie and her illegitimate baby were not welcome to join them. Emily-Elsie rented a room for herself and two-year-old Dolly in Lisson Grove. On May Day 1912 she met Daniel Kingham in his guise as Jack of the Green. At first he frightened her. Then he made her laugh.

Daniel, the house painter, once a plumber's mate, led the chimney sweeps round Lisson Grove. *I take my place at the head of the procession as those black-faced boys stand and stare. For this is how we do it, boys!* One of the sweeps had his blackened face smeared with white paint. 'As a child,' he told Daniel, 'I was kidnapped and sold to the sweeps to become a climbing boy. I've long since lost sight of home.'

Daniel took mystery very literally.

'Where is this home?' he asked the sweep.

'Some way beyond there,' the sweep said, pointing towards Paddington Station. Daniel was determined to make something of nothing.

'West of the sun and east of the moon!' he mused. The sweep shrugged and looked away. But Daniel was convinced he had hit upon something. He made a mental note to jot it down.

Daniel had a taste for Ye Olde England. I could hear him reciting penny ballads and folk songs. Emily-Elsie heard the jingling of bells and laughter. She went downstairs to investigate. Mrs Bonangelo, who spoke no English, pulled Emily-Elsie on to the door-step to have a look. She was laughing at the fellow prancing in the street, sheathed in ivy. He was a living beehive, a dancing pyramid, jigging up and down Lisson Grove. It was May Day and Mrs Bonangelo lifted up her petticoat to join in the dance.

They danced rustic fashion – knees and elbows akimbo, jagged beats. Their yells and contortions alarmed Emily-Elsie as did a man got up as a woman. He was large like a comic character in a ragged, ill-fitting dress, a wig made of tow, and brawny arms brandishing a tattered parasol. The Lady came prancing up to Emily-Elsie, calling, 'What have you got for Jack of th' Green?' Emily-Elsie bolted down Bell Street. But the dreadful creature, grinning like a satyr, followed her dancing and entreating till she reached the door of the cottage. Emily-Elsie bolted up the stairs and found Dolly, still asleep where she had left her tied to the bed.

Thaw with your eyes the frozen street,
Or cool my hot desire,
I burn within, although my feet
Are numbed for want of fire.
Thrum, thrum, thrum, thrum,
Come, come, come, come,

My dearest, be not coy,
For if you are (zit, zan, zounds) I
Must without your favours die.

Emily-Elsie cleaned and washed in the wealthy part of Marylebone. It was casual work paid for by the day, and she brought home 3s a week. To get more, she had to work harder. A midwife cost 10s, and her parents would not have her. So when her time came, it was the workhouse for Emily-Elsie. On the Spike (what the regulars called it), each infant was allotted 2s 11d per week for food. This was more than Emily-Elsie could scrape together, so she found herself on the Spike – a miserable place. One particularly cold winter, there were at least one hundred children on Dolly's ward. Her head felt light and draughty because the nurse had cut her hair. All the children had shorn heads. Their shouts rang against the walls and bounced against her ears. But Dolly lived in a hazy, muted realm where words had lost their bearings and had no meaning.

When they let her out, Emily-Elsie had found a room in the Sweetness and Light Cottages on Ranston Street for 3s 6d per week. She was always behind with the rent, and suffocated by the scent of condescension worn by the landlady. Miss Sims was a tall, rich woman who kept the rent in a bag with steel chain handles threaded through her belt. She tutted and talked about the 'deserving poor'. Emily-Elsie told her she was a widow. Woodlice and snails crawled up the walls as Emily-Elsie told her terrible, sad story. It was always dark in here even with the gas lights on. The two women repaired to the street outside. Dolly followed her mother downstairs, clutching her skirts. On the doorstep, she turned her back on the wavering signs of sympathy in Miss Sims's face. She sensed her mother's desperation, and fixed her eyes on the sunflower stamped above the doorway. The glaze had cracked. The cat-meat man was whistling down Ranston Street, carrying a pole on his shoulder with haunches of flesh dangling from it.

'Me-e-at – cat's – me-e-at.'

Miss Sims flinched at the sound of him. Dolly turned to contemplate her discomfort.

Emily-Elsie was a very busy woman. Dosing Dolly with Godfrey's Cordial; leaving her with the Eye-ties downstairs; scrubbing flagstones, washing and drying the breakfast dishes; filling the coal scuttles from the outhouse; cleaning the fire irons with an emery cloth, black-leading the fire grate; dusting, cleaning and polishing the cutlery and ornaments; beating and shaking the carpets in the courtyard. Begging. Pawning. Moonlighting. Borrowing. Foraging. Stealing. Baking cakes that Dolly sold on the streets for pennies. She sat on the corner of Ranston Street and Bell Street like a guy with a sign round her neck. *1d each*. Passers-by laughed and ruffled her red curls. Doing the hokey-pokey, Emily-Elsie was beginning to make ends meet, and Dolly was out of the workhouse more than she was in it.

The passers-by on Edgware Road were smiling in sympathy.

Like a jack-in-the-box, he sprang from behind the door of the Green Man. In a breach in the ivy, she saw dark curly hair with silver slinking through it, and a flash of eager brown face. He vibrated with energy as he leaned towards her. She shrank from the stench of his breath. Emily-Elsie was small and bundled with insecurities that gave her a certain charm. She had had a child already. The child trailed behind her, wearing her coat of shame. In the mornings, when Dolly watched her mother, all she could see was long black hair being punished for its lustre. Her mother raked thick strands of it across her scalp into a tight fist at the back of her neck. Then she scraped Dolly's bright, brand new curls back from her face. Dolly did not wince though she felt the pain.

'All you that inhabit squares and great streets,' Daniel shouted, 'for God's sake, give us money!'

The Lady laughed, and the circus followed. Emily-Elsie laughed and Daniel had found a companion.

I first heard about my great-grandfather from Dolly. She captured my imagination with stories of a man who wore a straw hat, lived in Paddington and died on Bonfire Night. Daniel Kingham was born in Tom's Court, off Duke Street, Mayfair, in 1878. His father, William Kingham, was a wine bottler from Paddington. Daniel spent his early childhood with his mother Annie's family in their mews house in Mayfair. They had once been servants for one of the great families of Grosvenor Square.

I followed his progress from Mayfair down to Oxford Street and then left at Marble Arch on to Edgware Road all the way to Paddington Basin where, beside the Grand Union Canal, I kept returning to begin and end my journey. There are rings of beer on every alehouse table west of Duke Street, and Daniel left them there. In a sly, gloomy corner he sat chewing on baccy and gossiping with totters. He loved tales of mishaps and malevolence. He had some form. But he was not guilty. 'On my grandmother's life, I longed for the other place. I drew plans of it, and conceived the signs. But by the light of day the only traces left were in the grate.'

Daniel came from a city that before the Great War was a cold, grey place where country folk brought their customs with them. The fair, granted by James II, was held on the east side of Hyde Park on 1 May each year and lasted for about a fortnight. It was a pleasure fair, with rope-dancing, wood-carving, and duck-hunting. The nobility came to Mayfair to behold the city at play. Daniel's grandmother, who was born and bred here, told him about the Star Ghost carawan where she got her blood froze for a penny, and the big-headed child and the livin' skellington where there was a Kaffir eating live rats.

At the end of a narrow cul-de-sac the door of 6 Tom's Court opened on to a common room. Nanny Allum was boiling the copper, and minding the babies. She was a Poor Law nurse so there were plenty to keep her grandchildren company. Two men sat in overcoats that were past their prime either side of the hearth.

'I'm thirsty,' said Salmon. These are my future cronies. 'Therefore I buy a pint of porter.' This is where Daniel learnt the art of self-deception.

'You're thirsty,' said Grogan. 'Therefore you have 7d.'

'Here's to your health,' said Salmon. The porter was sour but potent. He made a long noise as if releasing air from his lungs. Daniel was fascinated.

'*Litotes!*' demanded Grogan.

'It can do us no harm,' complied Salmon. He drained the pot of thick black liquid to its dregs.

Grogan caught the wide-eyed stare of a little boy. He leaned over and put his face close to the child.

'Do you know what I am going to tell you?' Daniel watched the wry mouth. A parched white tongue was molli-fying the lips. 'A pint of plain is your only man.' Daniel thrilled to the sense of revelation, the hint of things to come. *What pipes and timbrels? What wild ecstasy?*

'I never drinks anything but the most bestest gunpowder tea,' said Nanny Allum. Now it was his grandmother talking to him. Rarely did Daniel muster so much attention. His head was reeling with it. 'It does wonders even for the most screw-tiating cold.' She poured smoking green fluid from the copper. A fire spluttered throughout the year, and boys and girls sprawled in its feeble glow, playing with marbles and cats.

'I've got babies in me arms, babies up the stairs and all along the corridor, wrapped up in little beds and quietened down.' A flask of gin and a spoon hung from her belt. 'And other people's tots hanging on to me. It's a full house!'

Nanny kept the babies in the upstairs corridor, which she patrolled with her flask and spoon. Sometimes the babies all lined up in their cribs turned to look at Daniel. The older children poked tongues at him when his nanny placed him in a bundle of cats. Daniel found it hard to overcome his nervous distaste at their rowdiness. His mother Annie, who was gentle and too in love with her husband to notice, walked to William Kingham's place of work every day to take him his dinner. William returned each night to Mayfair from the industrial wharves of Paddington, by way of Hyde Park, soiled, dark and driven. There was a sharp-edged vapour to his clothes, and a smattering of sand that blew along the canal as though from a land of pyramids and sphinxes. Nanny Allum made a play of wiping the dirt from him. O! it was very dark upon the water, and bitter bitter cold! William said nothing. His first child with Annie had come too soon for them. Annie had been only sixteen. A year later, they married and Daniel came.

Daniel was watching his older brother. He saw Frederick's green eyes following Nanny Allum round the room. She stopped to mop Pappy Allum's chin with her apron. Pappy was old as the hills, but hills that had subsided into a rush chair that sagged to the floor. It took a chain gang of older boys to lever him out of it. Pappy had once been a liveried servant for a lord and lady. Now that he was old, he earned pennies as a road sweeper. But he refused to hold out his hand for the pennies. He stood by the kerb as though still waiting at table.

'Now, Pappy,' said Grogan, 'tell us how to hold a plate at table.'

Pappy smiled the blank smile of deep reverie.

'Heh heh,' laughed Salmon, growing sly. 'He's the cat that has the cream.'

Sometimes if the children cried loud enough and Pappy could find his *Treasury* in the tangle of straw, he would read verse aloud to them. Tonight his nodding face was unassailable. Daniel gazed hard at his grandfather, trying to divine the source of his calm. In the search for entertainment, Grogan stirred Pappy to speak.

'Some stick it between the frame and the back of the chair, which is an excellent expedient, where the make of the chair will allow it.'

Game over, Nanny's lodgers exited laughing. Nanny took Daniel and Frederick aside.

'Wait till their return later tonight.' She wagged her finger. 'The remorse will come upon 'em sumfin' terrible.' She sighed. But mostly, Nanny Allum told her boys stories about Orion. She sat up late to watch the stars crossing the sky, because, she believed, her own grandmother was situated somewhere in the Belt. Once she let Daniel watch them with her. This was the glory of his childhood. There was no one else there; Frederick was sleeping with their mother. Together with his grandmother, just them two, he looked out of the window of the second floor. Opposite was a new tenement with four floors. Its straight lines ran sheer towards the sky. The smooth red body of a wall-face, the curving grooves of an internal walkway, the regular rhythm of tiles and masonry soothed him as a mother would who returns to quieten a fretting child. Her own father, Nanny told him, was a well-born man, lived in a castle as draughty as a tree. At every sunset, it fell into the river, and scaly fish with eyes that bulged swam through its walls to stare at you. Nanny Allum's face was round, red and clean, her eyes soft and dusky blue. Daniel touched the kiss-curls on her forehead wondering that she should let him.

Frederick, her favourite, went very pale when Daniel gripped his throat with both his hands.

'Here was our comfortable English home invaded by a cuckoo. That was our situation, as told to me by my own nanny in the Belt. Whoever heard the like of it? In the nineteenth century, mind: in an age of progress?'

Pappy nodded. Frederick, a future King's Counsel, sat at Pappy's feet.

Twenty years later, in 1899, Daniel Kingham was arrested. This was a lead I could not resist. There was even a front-page headline: *Plumber's Mate in Fatal Brawl*, and a report in *The Times*. The fight took place on the Easter Bank Holiday weekend. Outside the Apollo Public House in Paddington Street, Daniel Kingham delivered the fatal blow. This was my great-grandfather and it seemed he was drunk and disorderly. Here was a relative to whom I could relate. What was more, he was on the fringe of a rags-to-riches story that would grace any penny ballad. Daniel's brother, Frederick Kingham, started his working life as a clerk for a famous barrister in Middle Temple. Frederick rose from the same poverty as Daniel to become King's Counsel in 1915, and a pillar of respectable society. Daniel, after being found Not Guilty, settled back into the slums.

Daniel was a drunk and a malcontent. 'My wife left me. My brother did me some small service. But I am innocent. I see what awaits me in my father – the trudge, the smallness of it.'

Daniel wanted more. He was like me. He told Emily-Elsie what happened that night at the Apollo. 'It was Easter Monday. I stood up and sang for the occasion. It was music night, after all. "Come all you young fellows, give an ear to my song; I will tell you of the story that will not take you long." White and his brother came in – they began to jangle. The landlady went round and told them to leave the house – they went into another bar – she told them to leave that – White pushed me back into my seat – I said to the others that I was surprised that Haynes, with a horse and cab, should want to quarrel. I said to them both, "It is holiday time; do not let there be any rowing."'

The trial took place at the Old Bailey. The charge was manslaughter (his brother's work). He wore his best suit. The reporter in *The Times* described him as a 'respectable young man'. The fear was palpable – in the cell, in the dock, in chains, in the dog house.

Witness for the prosecution: 'I am a stable man, of 47 Lisson Street, Marylebone. On Easter Monday I saw this quarrel; I saw the four men outside the Apollo fighting. Daniel Kingham crossed the road, and struck White a swinging right-hand blow which knocked White down. I followed Kingham and took hold of his arm. I said, "Come back." He said, "Leave go, or I will set about you."'

Louis Haynes, witness for the defence: 'I remember going into the Apollo on this day; Daniel Kingham was there. The Whites came in and then left. We went outside, and as I was getting into my cab White rushed round the corner and dealt Kingham a blow, which knocked him down. He fell on top of Kingham and kept on hitting him. I said, "Let him get up," and White said, "I will serve you bloody well the same." He came for me, and struck me a blow that knocked me down. When I got up I saw White on the ground and Kingham walking away from him.'

Daniel Alfred Kingham, the prisoner: 'I am a plumber's mate. I am twenty-one – I have never been in any trouble or fight before. I dispute that I struck the deceased a very violent blow – I was very excited and dazed. I had been drinking, but I knew perfectly well what I was doing. I walked away after it; I was arrested at my house, where the police found me.'

They came to the door of a model tenement block where Daniel's parents, 'respectable poor', were bringing up their children to better themselves. Daniel's uncle, the plumber to whom he was apprenticed, lived a few doors down. The building had rules: tenants were chosen from those judged likely to pay the rent and unlikely to cause trouble. I remember the few times the police came to Cameford Court. Once, they came looking for my uncle who had crashed his E-type into the shop front of Radio Rentals on Streatham High Road and left it there. My mother was tight-lipped and furious. My father did not say a word. Shortly afterwards I was arrested for shoplifting, Dolly was remanded for loitering, and my father left for Africa.

Not being a gentleman by birth, Daniel had no good introductions, and after his appearance at the Old Bailey, he took to spending time alone. He noted down the events of each day: *Cloudy, foggy weather at Brazen Head and Green Man, Edgware Road.*

'Has anyone heard the cuckoo? . . . It is well past Cuckoo Day.' There was seldom an answer that satisfied. *Sometimes at the cemetery I spot a woodpecker. I fancy yesterday I saw a swallow flying over Ha'penny Steps . . . . At about noon, a crowd gathers at Wharf Arms, Praed Street. Disperses at three. Evening: noisy and smoky. Night: sober with porters from the Great Western and others that have neither credit nor money. Broken promises and remorse. Sunrise: black coffee and water-gruel to be had at the Sally Army. Beggars take up position at Paddington Station.*

The wife he married before he met Emily-Elsie saw him puzzling over sigils and sums. These scribblings would surely indicate an escape route or do away with those who were harming him. Under the bed, they stored costermonger's potatoes in exchange for a sack or two. It was here she found *A disertation on the Ancient Mysteries, An explanaition of the sixth book of Virgil's Eneid, The matamorphosis and the Customs and Dogmas of the Druids*. But it was Freemasons who caused Daniel greatest concern. Who or what did they know? And had they had a hand in it? He was hearing boastful accounts of his brother Frederick that caused him to wince. His first wife left him for his best friend Louis Haynes. He hardly noticed.

When my mother left me at nursery school in the morning, I took this daily act quite literally. She had left me. I had lost my connection to a fragile, gauzy creature. In her absence, I was heartbroken. My sadness contained a guilty longing for a mother made of more stubborn material, who would withstand my demands on her time and body. From an early age, in the absence of a stable family member, I attached myself to a screen in our living room. My favourite times were summer holidays when I did not have to account for myself as my mother was out at work, and my father was somewhere in Africa – quite possibly dead. Dolly enjoyed these days, too. We watched *The Galloping Gourmet*, my first intimation of future intoxication taking the guise of fine dining. But my favourite programme dated from an earlier, more innocent time, an idyll within my childhood, which re-emerged in memories already tinged with nostalgia featuring a girl called Tiger. She shared a secret hideaway on a London Routemaster bus with other boys and girls. It was the bus that entranced me. Boarding it was like being granted free admission to a museum of lost objects that could be touched, handled and pocketed, no questions asked. There was such an abundance of curiosities. As well as these were antique road signs – I read them as Kabbalistic pointers to otherworldly adventure. The only adult in attendance was a harmless road sweeper happy to float on the tide of chaos generated by a pack of unsupervised children. Tiger had freedom of the city and access to an unregulated past. Dolly had this, too. Unlike Tiger, though, Dolly had the stain of poverty on her. Her clothes were crumpled and her tights were torn. Once the television flatlined, she slept on a folding chair in the living room, like a guardian of the tomb.

She carried within herself the stoicism of abstention. We walked for miles, my great-aunt and I, through south and west London and back again. She frightened me but she made me laugh when she urinated in the street and then walked on. She had no regard for convention. When Dolly did not sleep on a folding bed in Streatham, she slept in the open air of London's parks. Sometimes, when she left and I did not know where she was going, I would insist on winding her scarf around her throat and buttoning her coat for her. It was as though I knew that Dolly was open to the night. She left me to read poems about the pale moon and frozen dew, the shadows and the chill that visited this ageing, incontinent *Beata Beatrix*.

PART TWO

SUMMER 2008

Chapter Ten

WATLING STREET OR THEREABOUTS

One day in the summer of 1971, my parents took me to an adventure playground. We watched children climbing rope ladders and swinging from trees. We had recently returned from Freeport, Grand Bahama, where my father worked in a casino. I was six years old. We stood on the periphery of a South London playground united in not knowing how to join in. Our silent incomprehension stretched into long, isolating minutes. Still in silence, we turned our backs on the playing children, and returned to my father's oversized American Dodge, so at odds with our cramped flat. My parents' bickering resumed. Once home, I switched on the television.

For entertainment, there was always the street, which at night was lit by gas lamps. The sooty walls were fuzzy with phosphorescence. For long, waking hours, Emily-Elsie stood at the window watching the alley where urchins gathered. They whispered and conspired, and women stumbled after them. It was the children who interested her the most. She saw a boy each day, shoeless and hatless, her own age. He was playing catch with another boy and calling to yet more of them while his mother sitting on the doorstep looked on. The boy gathered up splattered plums from the fruit stall at Portman market. He brought them home bundled in his dirty jacket. Sometimes, after school, if her mother did not need her, Emily-Elsie followed him from a discreet distance, pulling her baby sister in a wagon. She was small for her age and dragged one foot behind her. He turned round and jeered at her. But she had found a way of not hearing him or the others.

Emily-Elsie Smith was born in one of Charles Booth's purple patches. Lisson Grove, then a subdistrict of Marylebone, was closer to Edgware Road than Regent's Park, and known for its rookeries and not its crescents. Lisson Grove, an area that had originally housed artists looking for rural peace, became home, from the 1820s onwards, to refugees from the potato blight. What had once been the final fattening fields for cattle being driven to Smithfield became camps for itinerant Irish. They lived in small huts set up in gravel pits, each hut boasting its own piggery and potato plot. Nameless, foreign creatures caked in the dirt in which they dug the tracks of the railway lived here in the Grove before it was developed to house city workers.

The houses were rapidly assembled as three-storey structures and crowded together in courts arranged around deep wells for water and open sewers for waste. Gardens were not supplied. Each house had a front door that opened on to a miniature hallway and a dining room. Stairs in the hallway led to a parlour above. There was also a bedroom on this floor for the parents of the house, and then up a further staircase two attic rooms: one for the servants and one for the children. The kitchen and work areas were in the basement. But those who could afford to did not want to live in an area so built-up or one that was known for its piggeries and itinerant Irish. Houses remained unoccupied before being sold to wilier landlords. The houses were then let and sublet until they were straining at the seams, and Lisson Grove became a slum almost as soon as it was built, rivalling the East End for notoriety, poverty and diphtheria.

'We come from Mah-le-bone,' Great-aunt Dolly told me. 'St Mary-le-bon,' this time giving the archaic pronunciation. She stood with her back to the gas fire; her feet planted firmly apart, hands clasped behind her back. Dolly was my introduction to English culture. I had an American accent, learnt in the expats' school in Freeport. She was a Cockney. It was imperative I learnt to speak correctly.

'The rain in Spain falls mainly on the plain.' Elocution lessons first given at Paddington Ragged School were passed down to me in the living room of our flat in Streatham. In this small, stuffy room, I spent what now feels like a seamless succession of summers lounging in sunlight filtered through net curtains. I conjured beaches that glistened with sand the colour of peaches and apricots, balmy weather, and water that was the clearest in the world with fabulous, friendly fishes. In the foreground, Dolly provided entertainment for a homesick child. She sang songs from her childhood and recited schoolroom litanies. She told me stories of endurance, larks and hardship, how she and her sisters tripped down Edgware Road in shoes with no heels to wash themselves in the public baths. They had 1d apiece for the purpose. They lived on a street that, as she told it, I illustrated with tottering arches, mysterious nooks and a crumbling staircase leading to a loft inhabited by conspirators. These were, of course, the Cato Street Conspirators plotting to carry out Guy Fawkes's intentions. They were before Dolly's time but they set the temperature.

Emily-Elsie grew up to wash her children's clothes in a big copper basin in the basement of another tenement just off Edgware Road. Dolly and her siblings sauntered round the warehouses surrounding Paddington Station in the hope of finding firewood, and any windfall. There were hedgerows along the towpath right up to the Ha'penny Steps turnpike where they could pick blackberries. Edgware Road was still referred to as Watling Street and there had once been a vast forest that covered the whole of west London. When a track was cut through the bottle-green peaks and shades of sage and broom, Watling Street emerged. It became a path that ran to Wales, and then the Romans paved it, joining it to their other marching route, Uxbridge Road. These two roads were inducements for wanderers to fix an abode amongst the coverts and lairs of Middlesex Forest. Wild boar and maybe even bears roamed the area; hermits foraged for fruits and twigs for fire, and witches boiled cauldrons in caves. Dolly's childhood, it seemed to me, was spent in a magical land, which, even as she reached maturity, was receding into the distance. But she brought it close to me.

Every day, her beloved mother, Emily-Elsie, trudged the great, paved length of the Edgware Road with the painful, forced step of one who has already walked far so that she could earn a pittance and bear the weight of her dependants. She longed to be free, so twice, thrice or four times a year, she drank whisky. It was her favourite drink, but the relief was momentary. By the time Dolly came to live with us she had nowhere left to go. Every time she mentioned her mother, her watery eyes longed to let go their tears. Her strident Cockney voice dwindled into a stubborn, silent requiem.

I was growing practised at watching children playing. Our front door opened on to a communal balcony that overlooked the forecourt of a council estate. Even though we, too, paid rent to an unknown landlord there was an unspoken injunction that the occupants of Cotton House were council tenants and thus not to be approached or acknowledged. I watched the forecourt at twilight from behind the concrete sweep of our balcony. Adults were coming home from work and children were throwing balls to each other, running up and down staircases, singing, shouting and chasing each other. On Guy Fawkes Night, there was a fireworks display. Crowds of children and adults gathered around a bonfire in the forecourt. My parents and I stood on the balcony of our privately rented flat before going back in silence to the television inside. I was relieved. On the balcony, I had felt the incongruousness, the sadness of our position, and I felt guilty for not being more like the children on the council estate, for not being able to make my parents happy. I found it easier to ruminate and read unobserved.

Sedate, suburban Streatham, which was safer than neighbouring Brixton, was very quiet. My father worked nights at a casino in Paddington. He was used to people noticing his dark good looks, silk shirts and gold chains. He had a mechanical contraption that released cigarettes like greyhounds from a trap when he flicked his soft pack of Camels. He was a glamorous man for such a small location. Streatham was too small for Dolly, too. She was used to the endless drama of subsistence, the hustle of Edgware Road, and its comforting river of unknown and unknowable passers-by. People who lived in Streatham were neither poor nor glamorous but relatively affluent, and when they did come out of their houses, greeted each other politely. The streets, as we walked them, were more like slopes and crests than thoroughfares or alleys. They were strangely unpopulated, and seemed permanently to bask in crêpe de Chine sunlight. There was a sense of order in the avenues of Streatham, and a sense of homecoming in their gardens that signified an end to life's struggles, and a mellow acceptance of the routine of maintenance.

Streatham's peaceful householders held little interest for us. They had no narrative. Their peace was a kind of death. But, for me, the reasoning behind the fading out of Streatham's residents took on a particular urgency. Locked in with my mother's unhappiness, I had found an escape route. It was a tunnel that led me down a series of neglected avenues that led off Streatham High Road. They were developed in the 1880s as part of an estate for workers with aspirations. Rich russet brickwork and terracotta tiling, mini turrets and spires, leaded windowpanes, an alcove doorway that recessed into darkness. An imaginary uncanny spectre was beckoning me into the silence and gloom of these avenues. I could not keep my fascinated gaze from seeking it out. One after another, these houses dipped in aspic, or captured in sepia, kept me going. It could only be a matter of time before one of the doors opened and I was invited in. A magical, upside-down, topsy-turvy land. I airbrushed passers-by in their casual high street clothes out of my meanderings, preferring to stay in a kind of reverie where nothing or no one could reach me because I was endlessly sustained. Soon it didn't matter if it was Victorian Gothic, art deco cool, or the haphazard arrangement of prefabs with vegetable patches that made the South Circular look so messy. I walked the streets by day and dreamt about their stretches lit up at night. I watched the shadows lengthen. I read books about children who had adventures. I lived in my own carefully tended and securely guarded private property.

It didn't occur to me that I was unusual. But I had an outer-body sense of myself as being apart and separate, unsure of my capacity to take up space unless it was in another sphere. It seemed to me that the children from Cotton House and the children Dolly told me about could go anywhere, and play with anyone they pleased. They could run in and out of each other's homes. They could eat at any time – asking the baker for leftover loaves or scavenging speckled apples from market stalls. It didn't matter if they went barefoot or got dirty, or if they sang rude songs and shouted. For me, it was important that I was well behaved because that kept my parents happy.

One summer day after school, I made friends with a boy my own age. He was playing with a ball and racket against the wall of the Baptist Church that separated Cameford Court from Cotton House. I was ten years old, but I knew even then that he was the most beautiful child I had ever seen. His skin and hair were the colour of Gale's Honey, his eyes were sage green, and his soft, Afro curls sprang from his head like spun sugar. Like me, he was quiet and polite, but eager for friendship. We discovered very quickly that we both liked tennis, and that we preferred Arthur Ashe to Jimmy Connors. I knew my mother disapproved of Arthur Ashe. He had made a Black Power salute when he won Wimbledon. I, on the other hand, admired his gesture of defiance.

The next day, the beautiful little boy brought another racket and waited for me to return from school. We resumed our conversation and started to play tennis against the wall. Just as I was getting into the swing of it, my mother came to find me. On seeing my new 'half-caste' friend, she called me away and looked grimly at him. I never saw him again. No matter how many hours I spent watching from the balcony, it was as though he had never existed.

*   *   *

From my porthole I watched my cats climbing in the branches of the willow tree. In the cramped darkness of my listing boat I held a piece of paper that gave me roots. But it seemed the only voices that could console me were the voices that weren't really there.

George could not call it waking up. It was more like coming round from a blow to the head. He did not know where he was, where he had been or what had happened. He forced himself on to his elbows, waited for the dizziness to pass, and peered into the darkness. Through the ragged cloth at the window, he could see a grey mist creeping into a small, shabby room. He was lying, fully dressed, across a broken bedstead strewn with rugs and sacking. Attempting to clear his head, he drew air into his lungs. The sharpness of the fumes he inhaled was such that he fell back on to the bed. For a moment, it occurred to George that he might be in the infirmary. A man he vaguely recognised and a large, haggard woman sprawled across the bed either side of him. But then, the irregularity of this arrangement startled him into recollection: the woman was Diamond Kate. On closer inspection, the other figure was his new brother-in-law, Herbert. Usually so vibrant and puckish, Herbert fluttered his eyelids as though he was in the grip of a fever. He was muttering in his sleep. With a shiver of distaste, George turned towards Kate. She had achieved the sitting position and was reaching for a tin mug on a washstand. She must have sensed George's gaze, because she turned round and croaked, 'Have another?'

Diamond Kate had once been an imposing woman, and a key member of the shoplifting gang known as the Forty Thieves. The kind of shops Kate's gang targeted were those found in high-class arcades around St James's. Kate was a convincing fake duchess – she used fur pelts as a smother. But she had another side to her. 'You see these diamond rings here,' she told her cronies back in the Grove. 'They'll take a copper's eye out in a single punch.' Kate's stature was to be her undoing. Shopkeepers could spot her a mile off, and loose talk from rival gangs got her caught. On her release from prison she could only find work as a prostitute's maid and police informant. When that work petered out, she ran a den on a street that looked like a scene from the Apocrypha. But a den was a den and business in Kate's den was good. She had reliable customers, and if there weren't enough Chinese about, she found a substitute for opium in the 'sweet vitriol' of her Irish homeland.

Herbert had never tried it. He had come to Kate's because she could fence some coal he had hoisted from the back of a cart. This evening she had a special offer on. He was in the process of sampling the goods when he noted with irritation that Cecilia was picking her way up the broken staircase, and sweeping her skirts over the nests of writhing bugs. She always seemed to know where to find him.

'Oh Herbert, you'll never guess,' she started, but the affront of the vapours was so startling, masking the sewers and cesspools, that she stopped. 'She's the prettiest little thing . . .' she faltered. 'An angel.'

Cecilia felt her eyes widen and a thirst develop. Diamond Kate was lecturing Herbert on the uses of various black bottles, an eggcup, a tablespoon and some tin mugs. Herbert was in no mood to listen to Cecilia.

'You rinse your gums first,' Kate directed him. Herbert washed his mouth with the brown water Kate had drawn from the standing pump. She continued her demonstration.

'It depends on the range of your potation,' she explained. Most females could only withstand a teaspoon at a time. Kate poured the liquid into an eggcup, and quickly, holding her nose, swallowed it. She gulped down more water.

'It lessens the burning,' she gasped. Cecilia had difficulty in swallowing it at all. Her eyes watered, her mouth closed in on it and the walls of her stomach contracted.

'It's highly provocative of vomiting,' Kate sympathised.

Herbert, however, had no such problems. After his table-spoon, he had felt his pulse quicken, his face flush, and a wave of hysterical excitement pass through him, before yield-ing to his own blithesome paradise. 'Ooh la!' he cried, his eyes glistening with love. Herbert was dancing at a ball and sipping fine champagne and flirting with fine ladies. Cecilia could only look on.

'Dip a sugar twist in it,' Kate advised, 'and see where that gets you.'

It got Cecilia, 'a married woman old enough to know better', said the Magistrate, wrapped round a lamp post with a police-man. Lisson Grove had become the Garden of Eden, and Cecilia was Eve in her undergarments, strolling around lamp posts that looked like trees dipped in black ink. She was transported, she told her sister, to a London where the walls weren't collapsing, the plaster wasn't peeling, the moon wasn't weeping and a person wasn't oppressed, choking on the miasma of a midsummer's night. Quite a crowd gathered to cheer the constable as he adjusted the hooks and eyes of Cecilia's gown. Once he had dressed her, Cecilia was ready to be escorted to Marylebone Magistrates' Court. Off he marched her to more cheers. Cecilia was glowing with love and laughter. Rarely had she felt like this. But she had known since a child that she had the capacity. Her mother had shown her such strange sights that she would never lose the wonder of them. The straggling band of dusty, ragged followers egged her on. She stopped the constable, curtsied to her admirers, and threw her hat in the air for an urchin to catch. From the window of Diamond Kate's garret, Herbert watched Cecilia being arrested. Kate beckoned him back in with a laugh – 'I bets you wish you'd never seed me!'

That night, across Lisson Grove, the stench of human waste was given a rinsing by Kate's stock of vapours. This, as she would argue, was the downside of supplying diethyl ether to her customers – the reek of it brought in the busies. But ether had outstanding selling points: small doses were needed for intoxication, it was easily obtained, and at a low price. What is more, Kate found she was profiting from an unexpected consequence of temperance campaigns. Swearing off alcohol was all well and good, but something had to replace it. The Salvation Army opened a shelter in Lisson Grove the year Emily-Elsie Smith was born. It was a one-stop shop for soup, soap and salvation. Every Sunday, Sally soldiers paraded the streets singing hymns and waving the Blood and Fire flag. Children danced in time to the beat of the drum.

Diamond Kate delivered Emily-Elsie in a tenement in Lisson Grove. The street on which this house teetered had been half swept away by the Great Central Railway. Navvies were employing the new construction method of 'cut and cover' to build tracks for the Metropolitan line. This would put Marylebone on the map. But for the poorer residents, the new roads and tunnels that cut through their courts and alleys forced them to crowd in even more.

The last house standing on Orcus Street was Emily-Elsie's first home. A broken-down cab, baskets of poultry, dung heaps, and costers' barrows were piled outside the front door, which was hanging off its frame. Emily-Maria Smith gave birth to her first child on the third floor. It was a quiet night so Diamond Kate came downstairs when she heard the telltale screams. In the one room occupied by George, Emily-Maria and soon-to-be-born Emily-Elsie were piles of wooden crates filled with onions, and a mattress to lie on. The onions were the wares by which George attempted to earn a living. They attracted roaches and bugs. There was no stopping them. You just had to put up with it. George was running his horse and cart without a licence. He could get caught at any time. This frightened Emily-Maria into a perpetual state of vigilance, a state of mind that was exhausting for her and George.

It had been a pregnancy punctuated by moonlight flits. Emily-Elsie emerged still in her birth sac – reluctant at least to leave that home. Kate punched it open and looked at the little blue face inside. She cleaned Emily-Elsie's nose and blew into her mouth. She pressed on her tiny, narrow ribcage. Emily-Elsie coughed and gave a yelping cry. She then took a deep breath and bawled. Kate cut the cord with her knife, and lifted the baby up to have a look at her. 'Rickets,' she proclaimed, and placed the baby on her mother's breast. While she waited for George to return from his daily round of job-hunting, Emily-Maria examined her daughter's legs and found that she could not forgive her midwife or the rest of her neighbours in Lisson Grove.

She explained to her daughter how they had come to such a pass. 'All our friends, Ma and Pa, cousins, family, all of them – tried to 'suade him to stop at home another year or two – and they're not badly off so they should know. But come he would, as if he must and couldn't help it, dear. I brought good clothes with us, dear, but they're all gone; and I'd be ashamed to go back so shabby.'

*   *   *

Emily-Maria and George had come to London from where
Emily-Maria's sister, Cecilia, had been sending reports of
prosperity since her marriage to a greengrocer in 1874. So
George and Emily-Maria had travelled by horse and cart to
Lisson Grove. Just as they had arrived, Cecilia had left her
husband and two sons for a rival greengrocer called Herbert.
He could do with a carman himself. Within the year, Herbert
had lost his shop to the Great Central Railway.

George was out of a job. Work was scarce. Stevedores,
carters and waterside porters, in particular, were 'the real
victims of competition', Herbert explained. 'Depressions in
trade weigh particular heavy on these occupations,' he sighed.
'But it will peak again,' he promised. 'I guarantee it!'

Herbert was born and bred in this warren of courts and
alleys, so George trusted him.

'Herbert has a different way of doing things,' said Cecilia.
'You'll get used to it.' Apart from the stench of the sewers,
there was something indefinable in the air. George caught a
whiff of it as soon as he turned his cart off Edgware Road and
into the Grove. When his horse nosed into what remained of
a terraced street, a delicious sensation swept over him.

'Emily,' he told his wife, 'I threw open my coat, put my
hands in my pockets, and lodged my old hat on the back of
my head.'

'Oh, George. Be careful.'

'And then I started to whistle!'

Herbert slapped George's shoulder in congratulation. 'Fay
ce que voodrah, mon frère!'

This carefree swipe soon translated into Do What You Can
To Survive. Everyone else was. Road sweepers, cadgers,
beggars, luggage-porters, thieves and prostitutes, as well as
carmen and their wives, lived for 1d per night upon the bare

boards or 3d per night upon a mattress. Despite the cheapness of their dwellings, George and Emily-Maria could not keep up with the rent. They moved around a lot but always stayed within the square mile of the Grove. Sometimes they had one room in a tenement, sometimes two. If they had a second room, George would let it out at a profit. Sometimes he let out one half of their only room if that was all they had. It made sense to stay in the Grove, on the grapevine, that way they wouldn't miss out on vital information. They needed to know where to go for cheap food or fuel, which shopkeepers would give them credit, where they could get childcare or give it, what firm was taking on hands, how to get a hospital letter and what strings might be attached. They had three more babies. As long as they stayed in the Grove they could just about subsist. Hungry children were always given meals, and the starving could always secure help from the neighbours, because the poor never knew when their turn to starve might come. Emily-Maria despaired. It was as though this area had walls round it. Once you were in, there was no way out.

The streets and green spaces of Paddington radiate outwards from the Basin. The Paddington arm of the Grand Union Canal, which passes through Southall and ends at Slough, starts its journey here. Along with the canal and the railway tracks, came wharves, warehouses, loading bays and tenement blocks. The day Emily-Elsie's youngest sister was born, 15 August 1895, a man with a pancake face was striking along Praed Street on wooden stilts. He was higher than the lamp posts that Aunt Cecilia would be dancing around that very evening. It seemed to Emily-Elsie as though everyone in Paddington was celebrating. The landlord of the Grand Junction Arms was emptying a pail of slops into the gutter.

'How's the missus?' he shouted.

'She's having it now. Got her sister with her.' George was sitting on his cart, his eyes following the circus parade as it brushed past him and Emily-Elsie. He would have to wait for it to pass. The horse dropped its blinkered head, unmoved by circus distractions. Emily-Elsie was transfixed. There were clowns in silk padded costumes. There were horses in ribbons and harness doing fancy steps in time to a flute and drum.

'They do eat up money,' said the publican, ignoring the parade because he'd seen it all before. 'Don't do nuffink but eat and wear out clothes.'

These horses were not like the large piebald her father kept, Emily-Elsie noted. These were silvery prancing creatures pulling a gilt-edged coach with a little girl inside. She looked like a fairy. George looked down at his own little girl – her eyes were circles of wonderment. She was small, even for a Smith, and she stood at a list. At seven, she had a face that was older than her body. Emily-Elsie cringed under her father's scrutiny. She hated to be looked at. She knew her leg was bad, that she was dark as a Gypsy, and that there was something not quite right in this.

'I'd like my girls to be quiet, homey girls, not like these flighty types, all frills and tight lacings.' Not like Aunt Cecilia, was what Emily-Elsie heard.

'Yes, George,' said Emily-Maria, 'and you'll have retired by then, you'll see, and we'll have a little place back at Ware, you can sit in the garden come the evening . . . I heard of a feller worked the dust and retired with fifty a year. It's saving what does it.'

George and Emily-Maria reckoned their daughter's darkness was due to the Baldocks on his mother's side.

The Baldocks, it was said, could trace their line of agricul-
tural labourers all the way back to the Templars. 'Baldac'
was the name of a Far Eastern city where genii lived, and
Aladdin had adventures, and from whence the Templars
came. This accounted for Emily-Elsie's black hair and
eyes.

The sight of a pretty circus child in her pink gauzy tunic
was just the beginning. Wings of net and wire arched from
her back. The reddest curls Emily-Elsie had ever seen bris-
tled like a halo around her head. Four French poodles
succeeded her. They pulled a tiny cart like as like to Pa's.
Only there were sacks of coal in Pa's. Then, more massive
than Paddington Station, making Emily-Elsie yell and
George gasp, a pair of elephants in single file, with golden
cloths and saddles on their backs. A great, stern-looking man
– just like a genie! – rode the first elephant. Emily-Elsie
shivered at the sight of him. Behind his great grey creatures
were throngs of people in fantastic clothes. A bewitching
procession of velvets, tinsels and satins that, while it passed,
was like living a dream. When it turned the corner on to
Edgware Road, Praed Street was bare and brown again.
Emily-Elsie looked down the long rows of two- and three-
storey shops and business offices disappearing into the mist
of what she had heard called Bayswater. Nearer to home, the
Grand Junction Arms was the most familiar building to her
– she would sometimes get a jug for her father – but the
largest was Paddington Station, and next to it, the Great
Western Hotel. They were so grand and forbidding, she
hardly dared approach them. She felt more at ease exploring
the wharves on the undulating, high-walled street that was
her new home. Irongate Wharf Road curved round the
Basin like a question mark. Here, in the Basin – the terminus

of all that power harnessed by the canal – she felt invisible, free to roam. There was so much going on around the dust heaps and stables, the warehouses of Paddington Vestry's Scavenging Department, the carts coming in and out of Selfridge's goods yard, the lads filling bottles at Boldero's Wine Bottlers', and the coming and going of cargo from trains and barges.

Fol lol de iddy row dow row
Sing toodledy teedledy bow wow wow

It was a funny thing but nearly all the time there was the strain of an organ piece or a penny-gaff ballad playing in her head. No matter what she was doing or thinking, it was nearly always there in the background. Strains of music she heard seeping from the Grand Junction Arms, or the Brazen Head, or any of the other pubs that dotted her landscape and occupied her father's evenings. More recently it was a song sung by Mick the Tug that spoke of distant lands and walking on water. The canal, polluted by stockyards, dust wharves, and bargees' sewage, formed a large, fetid pool that practically lapped at Emily-Elsie's doorstep. Her favourite vantage point was the jetty. With Father gone to work, and Mother being tended by Aunt Cecilia, Emily-Elsie's sisters could wait. She skipped the length of it, and climbed down the ladder strapped to the slimy brick wall in her bare feet, nearly into the water itself. She jumped on to the hatch of Mick's tug and perched there. It was almost as though he had been waiting for her. Mick sat in the stern of his craft, eating his breakfast of cold coffee and herrings. He nodded a greeting and handed her a tin plate and dished some up for her. It was silver, slippery and wrapped in jelly. He gave her a mug of coffee as well. Emily-Elsie knew better than to say anything. She just let the boat rock as he lent on the tiller and began to sing to her.

> *Oh who will I take on the Irish barge?*
> *Oh who will I take?*

'Take me!' she said, and Mick laughed. From the hatch of his tug, while he sang to her, she could observe the yards on the other side of the Basin, which contained piles of cinders and manure, and coal pits. This was where her father disappeared every day – into a haze of ashes and coals. The two rooms into which he had moved his family were a step closer to stemming Mother's tears by keeping her busy with constant, futile dusting. Irongate Wharf Road was known as 'the home of the dustmen'. Emily-Elsie and her parents were out of the Grove and into the Basin.

On his nights off, rather than stay at home in Streatham, my father played after-hours poker at the Mint on Edgware Road. The Mint is now the Mirage, a private health club providing sauna and massage for gentlemen only.

'You know,' she repeated with a heavy emphasis, 'gentlemen only.'

I had been looking for information about the Mint, which I knew had once been the Red Lion Tavern, where Shakespeare is said to have acted. It was now the Mirage. Clarity dawned. This woman was not interested in Shakespeare's formative years as a strolling player or the social history of Edgware Road.

'I'm so sorry,' I said. 'I've made a mistake.'

'Oh, don't worry, dear,' she replied. 'We all make mistakes.'

I could hear a smile as she put the phone down, and then I felt its rueful amusement. It washed over me from head to toe: forgiveness from a woman who made it her business. I had to laugh at my benediction. I wanted to ring her back.

There was a thriving trade in prostitution very close to Emily-Elsie's home. The proximity to Marylebone and Paddington railway stations was vital to that trade. Brothels and disreputable houses made the Basin slightly shady and Emily-Maria fidget with a nameless anxiety. George rubbed shoulders with ladies of the night in the Grand Junction Arms. Although he was short in stature, his heavy shoulders and stout forearms told a story.

'All I have to do is keep watch in the doorways.'

'Of the old tenements?'

'That's it.'

'No one minds what anyone does there.'

'While the girls do business with the punters.'

'So you being there ensures they get paid for their troubles?'

'That's it.'

'Nice work, Georgie boy. A bob a go for nothing really, just standing there, and then, more than likely, a drink on top and something more.'

Cecilia also had a seasoned approach. 'Live and let live!' she declared.

It was only Emily-Maria who saw George's new position as a turn for the worse. Strangely, she could only feel anger towards her older sister. She might have known Cecilia would laugh it off. But then she had left her boys to go with Herbert, and he was twelve years younger than her. Emily-Maria watched in silence as Herbert and Cecilia led George a merry dance round sure-fire schemes and opportunities.

There was nothing she could do to stop him. So she kept dusting and cooking and worrying and cleaning and bearing children. At least only one had died.

This summer was different from any other time Emily-Elsie could remember. Nothing much had happened that she could explain in thoughts or words – true, her mother was having another baby. But this was a feeling of change. Ever since they had moved to the Basin, she had been excited. This particular morning she couldn't wait to get out of bed. After breakfast with Mick, she loaded Adelaide and Doris on to the wagon, strapped them into place to stop them falling out, and roamed the wharves. She was busy singing. Sometimes she filled her head by hatching plans. So absorbing were they, she would look up suddenly or be distracted by her sisters' cries, and realise she was in a part of the Basin she didn't recognise. North Wharf Road was full of dust heaps that rose like mountains. There were strange, dirty characters in long, flapping garments sifting through the foothills of each heap. They looked out from under their peaked caps with red, sore eyes and held aloft old shoes, bones and buckles. A bare-armed, grubby-white-aproned woman called out to Emily-Elsie from a house with broken windows patched with paper. Words Emily-Elsie couldn't distinguish were coming out of the woman's black mouth. Very scared, she turned tail, nearly ejecting her sisters on to the cobbles. She could hear the woman's laughter for days. This incident excited her the most. What would her mother say?

Just as she was imagining the scolding she would get, she ran into her father's cart. She was so busy plotting and planning, he had to grab her by the arm to make her see him.

Chapter Eleven

MY OLD MAN'S A DUSTMAN

By all accounts, 1976 was the hottest summer, although its stillness and heaviness spread through all my summers, none of which I remember in any meaningful detail. There are not many illustrative anecdotes because my childhood is cut off from me. I have this blankness in common with other addicts. We switched off early. However, I do remember sleepwalking between lessons at school. I must have taken part and completed essays and sums because I was considered clever at English and adequate at maths. I knew enough about sums to know there was never enough. Numbers equalled money. I remember stealing money from my mother to buy yet more sweets and Agatha Christies. I remember hoarding plastic bags and bus tickets under my bed. Sometimes I would get them out to contemplate the evidence of where I had been and what I had bought when I had been there.

My favourite part of the day was walking home from school. The freedom of release from captivity was celebrated outside Streatham Hill Bus Garage (gateway to central London). This was the start of a great adventure, where the girls who wore their ties unknotted lit up from packets of ten. I joined them by sucking on a cigarette-shaped sweet and trying to make them laugh. I was the class comic. I had a found a way through my dilemma. I also found the violin. I took lessons in a small house with a sensitive woman. She shared my appreciation of melodic yearning. She had a wrist permanently bandaged in beige crêpe.

'This is why I teach,' she explained, holding her wounded wrist for me to see. We played and swayed and talked about Schubert in a garret room with a slanting roof and lit by a gas fire. I loved the violin and Schubert in particular. One day I was so overcome with emotion, I fainted. My teacher was kind and looked concerned. Her kindness frightened me. In 1977, I was a twelve-year-old schoolgirl learning the violin and how to smoke. I couldn't do both – too much of a stretch in attitudes – so smoking won. Ultimately it was more effect-ive at stifling feelings that music stirred.

I narrowed my eyes so that I looked mean and wore heavy black eye liner and white lipstick. If the other girls found it hard to take me seriously, it was because I was always chang-ing. I started with Enid Blyton, and became head girl from St Clare's. I moved on to *The Lord of the Rings* in which Legolas took my fancy. Then my mother bought me a copy of *Bored of the Rings*, and Legolamb introduced me to parody. I became my own worst reviewer, mocking my every move. With a Pernod & Black inside me, I lightened up. Pernod & Black was like sucking on a sweet and went down easy. Speed gave me confidence to talk to boys who were foreign objects to be explored and then displayed like the badges and safety pins on my lapels. Me in punk mode went out with Matthew, who had the spark of unpredictability. Me in Mod Revival mode went out with his best friend, who was smoother. I swung between an original 1960s tube dress from Kensington Market, white tights and winkle-pickers from Carnaby Street, and dishevelled school uniform with monkey boots and neon ankle socks. My mother was generous with my clothes allowance, which was just as well. I felt like a rich woman with £20 per month on top of £5 per week pocket money. No wonder my Sunday morning job in a newsagent's did not last long. My first experience of work consisted of three mornings of incomprehension that I should be expected to do anything apart from arrive on time, and my employers' futile attempts to explain what they required of me.

The trouble with fixing on men, drink, clothes, food and money was that they were never enough. I always returned to my self, and an aching feeling of being empty. This was compounded when my father left 'for Africa'. This was all the explanation I needed. My mother's clarification was: 'He doesn't love me any more,' and this was overwhelming. Essentially, my father was a man to whom I had to say goodbye. At twelve years old, I was all for getting it over with. I waved him off from the balcony, and closed the door behind him. My stomach heaved, but there seemed no point in following this lunge into sorrow. Instead, I watched myself in the mirror smoking a cigarette.

It was at this time Dolly went out shopping and failed to return. I listened to my mother's conversations on the telephone, and heard that my great-aunt had been arrested for 'loitering with intent'. I asked my mother what this meant. It meant that Dolly had been sleeping in a shop doorway. I knew Dolly had form for shoplifting. So did I. But Dolly was compelled to steal for others. She left food parcels on 'poor people's' doorsteps. I did not see the depths of poverty that Dolly had seen but I did see my great-aunt Dolly. Her skirt was stained with grass and her shoes were worn to flaps held together by laces. This was the woman with whom I felt the bonds of mischief, gambling, madness and song. She was sitting on a bench outside my school. I walked straight past her.

My real friends – the ones I still idealise – were the quieter, more introspective girls who pursued extracurricular activities. But I had lost sight of them. It was their quietness that, like kindness, frightened me. Kindness contrasted too painfully with the voice in my head that was mocking me. Quietness emphasised that I was in a state of flux, aware that only a building or a tree could withstand this restlessness. In my loneliness, I thought this state of being was mine alone.

Emily-Elsie looked up at the angry wraith grabbing her arm and calling her by name, and hardly recognised him. When he had been a coal merchant's man, her father had been black from coal dust. Now he was grey from ashes.

George's brother John had arrived from Hertfordshire just in time to help George in his latest venture, dust-collecting. 'You're the filler. I'm the carrier,' George explained. 'Put this on.' He handed his brother the fantail hat of the London dust man.

George Smith had joined the highest echelons of London's legendary characters. Herbert and Cecilia laughed as George and his brother took their places side by side on the cart. 'There goes Dusty Bob,' Herbert laughed. George, the brunt of his joke, was too full of resolve to notice. His high box cart and his horse were all he required to make a go of it.

'Here comes Black Sal,' Cecilia rejoined as Emily-Maria came out to see them off.

'Dust-oy-eh!' Once the cart was full to capacity, they drove it back to the dust yard, where they unloaded on to the heap, received 6s, and then proceeded on their round. The trouble was, they were unlicensed, and then reported to

Paddington Vestry. There was a fine to pay, and Emily-Maria's hopes were dashed again.

Then George had a large consignment of coal to deliver to Portman Mansions in Baker Street. His heart was heavy because this load wasn't enough and his stomach was aching. But he also had some business to put Herbert's way. So he drove his cart in circles round the Grove, stopping off at beer shops and alehouses.

He came to a halt outside the Brazen Head and dismounted. Herbert was in the saloon and beckoned George over to the bar.

'I was just telling Bill here, about Portman. Do you know,' he asked before George could stop him, 'I saw him the other day outside the market with a big gold chain draped across his belly.'

'It makes yer sick,' said Herbert's drinking partner. ''E walks round 'ere like 'e owns the place.'

'That's because he does!' said the barman.

'He does indeed,' Herbert soothed. 'And do you know what?' he continued. 'That man waxes rich on the likes of us. We're the best-paying tenants in London. That we should pay so much for so little, and almost have to fight to get it, and then be exploited, is a disgrace. It's a disgrace, I say, to the government,' and he stopped. 'Another of your fine ales, my friend . . .'

The barman rallied.

'. . . which, by the by, is never tired of protecting the oppressed of all races that on earth do dwell . . .'

George had heard this before, and been much enthused by his brother-in-law's radical treatise. Today Herbert's thin moustache looked false as though it had been stuck on for fancy-dress. Too much had happened now to George and his family – there had been too many reversals of fate and fortune, too long an acquaintance with dirt and death. George wanted a way out and Herbert's rhetoric was wearing thin. If he spoke any faster his moustache might fall off and land in his pint of ale. George held up his hand as though to hush him. But Herbert's new drinking partner hadn't heard the speech. George had to swallow his frustration as a fist pounded the bar in applause.

'Yes,' said Herbert, 'all races that on earth do dwell, except those of that particular race who have the honour to be free-born Englishmen.'

And with this triumphant flourish, Herbert was assured of his next drink.

'It makes me mad,' said Bill, gesturing to the barman. 'The bastards who own these tenements are mill-yon-airs, I tell you, while what do you see walking around these streets? Hungry, worn-out doffers and ricket-legged kids. Don't it make you mad? Don't it?'

'Indeed it does, my good man,' said Herbert, edging away from the motes of dust flying off Bill's clothing. 'Now, George. What can I do for you?' and he took his erstwhile employee by the arm. Herbert was taller than George with a carefully studied air of good deportment. He put a convivial arm around the smaller man's shoulder, and they stood in the doorway contemplating George's cart.

'Well, Herbert, I've got a delivery to do and I've got my ticket from the wharf, but I've had a stroke of luck, you might say . . .'

'Is it coal, George?'

'Yes. The guvnor gave it to me this morning – "a one-off", he said, "for old times' sake", but I've managed to pick up some extra sacks . . .'

'Coals sold from the wharf are delivered in sacks of a hundred and twelve pounds. Right?'

'Right.'

'Well I can find a home for them. But there's something more we can do, Georgie boy. The seller's ticket states the weight of the coals. Right?'

'Right.'

'Well then, George. You've got your coals weighed. You've got your ticket, and you've got some surplus. You stay here while me and Bill lightens your load. Then you proceed.'

'But I need that five bob off you, Herbert. The horse needs shoeing, and he's really on his last legs. I don't know how I'm going to manage . . .'

'I know. I know. Howsoever, if I remember right, and I'm quoting now: if any purchaser requiring any sack of coals to be weighed shall find the coals to be deficient . . .' Lines of concentration creased his high, smooth forehead. 'And shall signify to the carman his desire to have all the coals reweighed . . .' He paused for breath and a glug. 'Then the carman shall remain at the house of the purchaser with such coals,' another glug, 'and the cart, etc,' he spluttered, 'until such coals are weighed.' He paused for dramatic effect. 'Et cetera. Now that's right, isn't it, George?'

'Yes, Herbert, but . . .'

'So what you do is: you delivers the coal, it gets weighed, it tallies with the ticket and you gets your money. Then you sends message back to the wharf that you've been delayed in the reweighing. In the meantime, me and Bill can shift your extra sacks and what with the sum you gets from the purchaser, you, me and the girls can do a runner out of here, and be gone by tomorrow morning – by which time it'll be too late. Now that's one in the eye for the man what's promised you a security and laid you off, ain't it, George? But notwithstanding the fittingness of this little venture.' He lowered his voice. 'I've got an opening for us, George. It's a new start, a fresh country, ripe for development, and it's just up your alley.' He nodded in the direction of Bill in his fantail hat and dirty breeches. 'Bill here's been telling me all about it. Southend, George, sur la mer!'

'But, Herbert, I've started saving.'

'It's no good saving, mate,' advised Bill, coming up behind Herbert. 'I saved for ten years and the savings bank went broke and left me nothing but a savings book for me trouble. Get a close tip and take a chance, that's the only system.' He took George by the elbow and led him back to the bar.

'That's gambling,' laughed the bartender.

'Well, sir,' said Herbert, licking his lips, 'it's a gambling game. Now if you would give my brother here a brandy and water, we'll be on our way.'

George took a sip from the glass proffered by the bartender, and his head cleared and lightened in an instant.

'I'll see you later, George,' said Herbert. 'Meet me at Kate's around lighting-up time. You know what to do,' and he led Bill out to the cart before George could think of a riposte.

'Right-ho, Herbert,' he said, addressing his brother-in-law's back. Whether out of insecurity or resentment or pure and simple talent for imitation, Herbert carried himself like a gentleman, dressed like a gentleman, and always insisted on being treated as a gentleman. What is more, on the whole, he got away with it. And what is more, George, the unemployed carman from Hertfordshire, could not resist the odds his brother-in-law put his way.

'"Okey pokey penny a lump, that's the stuff to make you jump."'

'What's that?'

'It's a song my great-aunt used to sing.'

We were celebrating the departure of Nancy's husband. He had paid a surprise visit that luckily caught Nancy alone.

'I played wifey,' she giggled, 'and we went to see his sister.' She switched to serious. I could only imagine the kind of encounter that must have been.

'Do you get on with her?' I hazarded.

'She is very proper.' Nancy sniffed, and that was that. Nancy lived in the moment and she rinsed it for all it was worth. We were doing cocaine on *Tempest* preparatory to a night out in the dens and dives of Southall. Nancy looked the part with golden and black curls, gel nails and demon lashes. I looked like her older, more sedate, pale-faced maid. No matter, this was a girls' night out. Pete was 'on a job in Slough'. Nancy's resident boyfriend, Leroy, was out for the count. Leroy was a younger black wannabe version of Pete. He dealt in Wake and Bake, the latest derivation of skunk.

'I got a bunch of new buds and some Sour D. Been bangin' all day. Just burned a couple of purp bongs . . .' and he keeled over on to *Tempest*'s bunk.

Sometimes Ecstasy did the job. 'Look, hon, the thing about E is that it doesn't freak you out like skunk does. Mind you, this Wake and Bake that's just come out, you can smoke it all day and still get stuff done, as long as you stay off the Sour Diesel. Yes.' Pete sighed, sensing the competition coming up behind him. 'Wake and Bake is the next big thing.'

Pete had got me a bag of pills from a carpet-fitter who had done a job in a dealer's house and had found half a kilo under the carpet. 'He must have forgotten about it,' said Pete. 'It's the good stuff, honey. I'll let you have a bag for a nifty.'

How could I resist? I was smiling in concert with the universe. I was refreshed by being amongst people. I watched

Nancy. 'I'm wigging out,' she laughed, and it was true. Her dance moves were such that her curls were sliding off her head. It was the first time I had seen her wigless. She looked like a beaming, shiny infant with nappy hair in cornrows. We laughed at Nancy's relinquishment of the vestiges of glamour.

It didn't last. Leroy, who had awoken from his slumbers, and was raging with skunk psychosis, had followed our trail around Southall. It hadn't been difficult – 'Trust me. Everyone clocks you,' Pete told me, 'and all the boys know Nancy.' Leroy found us in the back room of the Harvester. It was pounding with dub and sexual tension. He pulled Nancy off the dance floor by her plaits.

Most of Emily-Elsie's plans concerned how she could help her father and mother and sisters leave the Basin. She saw the barges loaded with dust that her father had helped to gather. She knew they were going upstream to Southall where the dust was turned into bricks. And the bricks came back to the Basin on more barges. She saw them come and she saw them go. But she wanted to go on a barge that sailed across the Channel that Mick told her about. Emily-Elsie's plans always had the same outcome. Each time, she found a pool of clear water in which she could wash her hair and her body, and come to the light fresh and shining.

George Bernard Shaw based *Pygmalion* on a story that shocked the nation. The scene is Lisson Grove, 1883: an undercover journalist has heard rumours of child prostitution. He scours the streets looking for a lead, and meets a chimney sweep willing to sell his daughter 'into service'. Nudge, nudge, wink, wink. Her name was Eliza Armstrong. She came from the Grove. It was a scandal, and Lisson Grove Lingo was part of the language. Lisson Grove Lingo, as spoken by Eliza

Doolittle in Shaw's *Pygmalion*, and my great-aunt Dolly when we were alone in the living room of Cameford Court, Streatham. It all came back to her: the piggeries, the Irish, Eliza Doolittle, Eliza Armstrong, prostitution, drunken debauchery, unwanted babies, diphtheria and open sewers. So much she could hardly bear it. But I was listening.

It was lighting-up time. Emily-Maria was in bed with a new baby in a room in which the ceiling was showing the laths above, and the floor had broken away in places. Its furniture was a dilapidated four-post bedstead, a chair and a deal table. A breeze came through the broken casement bringing in a blanket of noxious fumes.

'I'm calling her Daisy.' The baby that nestled in her mother's arms was wearing what looked like a cap of damp copper curls and squiggles. 'It's the reddest hair I've ever seen,' said Emily-Maria. Daisy opened her eyes, and an electric blue glint lit the gloom. Emily-Elsie saw the fairy in the gilded coach.

She crossed Edgware Road as though she were treading water, and wound her way back to the last house standing. There were loud voices laughing and shouting in the night air, heavy with a pungent fragrance. Aunt Cecilia and a constable were dancing. She saw her uncle's head disappear into the garret window. She saw her father's horse and cart outside the house where she was born. She took hold of the horse's head and jerked it towards her. The horse that had borne the weight of George's labours, weary of pulling its load, destined for the knacker's yard, parched mouth gnawing and desperate, was jerked out of its torment, and sharp yellow teeth snapped Emily-Elsie's arm.

Chapter Twelve

LISSON GROVE LINGO

'The werry best,' Pete whispered in my ear. His demotic was more dizzying than the skunk that had been harvested in an Essex warehouse. It gave me a shock, a thrill of excitement. His insinuating voice had opened a door for me that would surely lead to a world of lost and transposed consonants, where the wayward sons and daughters of Samuel Weller got up to all sorts.

'Seek and ye shall find.' He took the baton back again, sucked deep and sighed. It was a brief excursion into a Cockney conurbation, the world my mother and my great-aunt Dolly had tried to hide from me. Elekyooshun was the key to survival. Only infants who warble about 'wabbits' drop their labials: infants who don't know any better, crafty types who do, or drunks who don't care if they do or die. Dolly turned her nose up, and so did my mother, at any hint of dereliction. The trouble was they kept giving me glimpses of what they feared and then pretending it hadn't happened. Pete's misplaced 'w' was a staging post on my descent into a London that had always been pulling at my attention before vanishing like a scent borne on the air.

'The werry best.' He said it again, and winked at me. For a split second the idea flashed through me that he knew what he was doing; but that was the genetically modified weed supercharging my responses. Pete smoked a tenth a day.

'At £13 a tenth I don't see it as a bag of weed. I see it as thirteen Es that's gonna last me ten hours when I hammer the whole bag. You can't tan black or hash like that 'cause you'd gouch out. But six or seven spliffs of Wake and Bake, I can reach the same level as if I'd popped a pill.'

We stood where Babbu gave room for smokers to light up and review the rush of Orchard Street. The doorway of the Brickmakers' was the perfect place to lose my grip on consciousness. It opened like a gaping mouth on the corner of Orchard Street and Shackleton Road. A black space that exhaled straggling smokers and sucked them back in again. Behind me, from the depths of its internal workings, were the diffused strains of a perpetually wailing jukebox. The hush and backwash and echo made a sibilant ebb and flow. Calls and responses and competing beats and vibes cushioned the doubts and queries that assailed me. The faded assurance of leatherette banquettes, into which I could sink with decorum, disguised the sudden weight of my head and loss of blood to my legs. The more I smoked the more the view became riveting – worshippers headed to the golden dome of a Sikh temple – the largest outside India – and crack-heads hurried to the Shackleton Estate – so quiet and orderly, yet so notorious.

'There's Killer.' Pete pointed at one of the hooded men.

I asked how he got his name.

'Take a wild guess,' was my answer.

The night lights blurred and scowling faces loomed at me. One face in particular became more insistent. A pale, skinny girl in a slimy tracksuit was scurrying in and out of parked cars. The same girl with anxious eyes I had seen on the slot machines and then with Spider was now looking at Pete, who was standing behind me. She seemed to be seeking reassurance. I checked to see his response. He inclined his head in the affirmative, then looked away as though nothing had happened.

'Who's she?' I asked.

'A whore,' he replied, and went back inside. I followed him. Babbu's turban wagged behind the bar as his customers conducted their business just off his licensed premises. Crucial to his enterprise, they came back in to buy more drinks. His customers were skanks and small-time hustlers – elderly men who sold rocks and bags when they hadn't smoked it all. 'That ugly skank-a-dank took all my money,' I heard Elvis mutter when the girl in the slimy tracksuit slid past him at the bar. The first time I had seen Elvis I had been unable to stop myself recoiling in distaste at his obvious descent into destitution. Now I greeted him like an old friend. He was looking more and more like the cautionary ending to the tale of Huggy Bear. The 1970s were still playing in his head and he was a player running girls and blow. In reality he was subsisting on benefits, blazing rocks in a bedsit, chasing girls young enough to be his granddaughter, some of whom may well have been his granddaughter but who, anyway, tripped him up time and again. The girl in the tracksuit – 'She's changed her name to Carly,' snorted Pete in derision – looked back at me as she exited. It was as though she were sizing me up and making a mental note to work me later.

Sheneice and Son of Elvis made their nightly trip to the Brickmakers' just before closing time, which was when business started for them. Sheneice was eight months pregnant.

In repose, her face was sullen and mean. Although she was shorter than me, I shrank in her presence. She was ruthlessly muscular, and regarded me with unflinching blankness. I sank further back into the safety of the banquette. Under the neon strips that lit the pool table, she was whispering in Pete's ear. Each time he stooped over the table, she was standing behind him, and her gaze had not moved from my face. It was like being observed by cold fish eyes that calculate distances through a layer of transparent skin. Pete eventually shifted her by straightening up, putting his hand in his pocket, and handing her some small change. Son of Elvis was Sheneice's partner and the father of her unborn baby. He had just been released from Wormwood Scrubs and seemed still to be wearing prison sweats. He was probably just as dangerous as his mate but, playing off her 'bad cop' routine, he could afford a more jovial approach to intimidation. He shook hands with his father in a complicated exercise of high fives, and smiled graciously when I congratulated him on his own imminent fatherhood. 'I've got to find me some money to pay for it now,' he confided – looking me up and down.

And then that moment came again. We had all reached the same level because we had all had exactly the right amount of alcohol topped up with exactly the right quantity of drugs. 'I don't have a drug of choice,' Pete joked. 'I have no choice!' The jukebox chimed sweetly, the lights softened and we swayed in harmony. Even Sheneice smiled shyly at me. In this twinkling of an eye that had been chemically manufactured, I felt an alliance I hadn't felt before with the customers of Babbu's pub. We were an alliance of those determined to persist in our desire to desire. There was no pretence here. We were not drinking imported wines or beers in faux-rustic gastro-pubs (been there, done that). Nor were we experimenting with psychotropic substances (being stoned does not make me a shaman). We were honest and united in our desire to lose consciousness on a regular basis. Pete was our leader because he always kept his cool and stayed flush. There had been a time . . . but that was another story, way back when. He had returned from the brink triumphant and self-medicating. If everyone around him was freefalling into chaos that was their lookout. When Sheena let us know that she was clucking he tutted, relented, and bought her a brandy and Coke. It shut her up for as long as it took her to drink it. Babbu beamed as the next brandy and Coke was ordered and as though Pete were an errant son. To me, he was a relic I had found in a curiosity shop.

'I can't blame Herbert,' Emily-Maria told her girls. 'Nor Cecilia. But I wish they hadn't.'

'You know she's killed a couple of people,' he sidled up to me, insinuating.

'Who?'

'Sheneice. Who d'ya think?'

The shock was like a hit.

'She got away with it,' and with a wink he sashayed back to the pool table.

I prided myself that my nights out in Southall ended with me still standing. Once I was aboard *Adam Bonny*, the collapse began. My cats became used to the sound of sobs and wails stifled by pillows. They are discreet and forgiving creatures. One morning, though, a plaintive howling brought me round. It was Nellie. She was running in circles around me. I then realised I was on the floor of the galley kitchen in the foetal position. It wasn't just Nellie who was screaming.

Some nights suspicion, mistrust, obsession and terror clutched at my brain while I was still in the Brickmakers'. The Four Horsemen of the Apocalypse were in relentless pursuit of Pete's infidelity.

'Who is Carly?' I demanded to know.

'I've told you, honey, she's just a friend.'

The first time I walked into the Brickmakers' Arms I knew something bad would happen. I figured it would involve me getting mugged. In the depths of my addiction, the one thing I held on to above my health, safety, or that of others, was my money. I could not afford not to be fully self-supporting. To admit I wasn't would put me at the mercy of the machine. Pete needed to play women off against each other in order to create insecurities. That way, he didn't have to feel his own. His life depended on the people around him falling to pieces. Like me, Pete deluded himself that he was still standing. We were both standing in the gutter, looking down at those who were on their knees.

'Dad hasn't had a bath since Chelsea lost against Barcelona 5–1. That was in 2000,' pause to cue the ball, 'which explains the smell.'

'All right, love?' this mound of rags, sores and beard asked me. 'Fancy a drink?' he winked.

'Leave off, Dad,' snarled Pete. To my consternation, he was seeing his father as competition.

Quite often, I found myself vomiting with horror in the toilets of the Brickmakers' Arms. Then, brushing myself off, I tried to stay upright as I felt my way back to the bar.

Cecilia walked back from the Magistrates' Court, all the way down Edgware Road, because she did not have a penny for the ride. A small, bushy-bearded, bandy-legged man walked ahead of her. He had a bowler on his head that signified to Cecilia better times. There was something incongruous in its jaunty tilt that captured her attention. He did not look as though he had any reason to be jaunty. But there he was, right ahead of her, strolling along with his hands clasped over the tails of his greasy frockcoat, picking his way among the unseeing pedestrians, packing boxes and ferreting children. He walked without hearing their yells, or the clatter of the omnibuses, the cries of the hawkers and carters. Cecilia was vaguely aware of wanting to observe him further, at her leisure, and, somehow, to puncture his self-possession. She chose not to go back to the Grove where she lived with Herbert. She never knew what mood he would be in. Cecilia was unable to resist adventure but it had ended up with her in the Grove, longing for a bigger life. If only she could get to it. Herbert had promised he would get her there. Although she did not know it, she felt safer with her sister and George. So she turned left on to Praed Street, as did the man with the bowler.

The station generating steam and the passage of cargo, the bell-boys, the shops and warehouses open for business – all this commerce reassured her. All was right with the world. It had to be for all this to keep happening. She paused on the threshold of Praed Street to feel the length and breadth of it before she allowed herself to be carried by its forward motion. The hard blue sky had blanched the dirt and grime of the street. She began to hum a song she liked, 'Pretty Little Polly Perkins of Paddington Green'. The man ahead of her was clasping and unclasping his hands. She felt the laughter welling up in her – what a strange little party he was. He came to a sudden halt in front of a shop window. Cecilia stopped, too, to see him better. She was as bee-yoo-tiful as a butterfly and as proud as a queen. In profile, the small, threadbare man with bandy legs was gnawing his lips. A maidservant with an ankle like an antelope, the milkman laments. Polly gives short shrift to his proposal.

> 'The man that has me must have silver and gold,
> A chariot to ride in and be handsome and bold.
> His hair must be curly as any watch-spring,
> And his whiskers as big as a brush for clothing.'

Polly dreams of marrying a Wi-count, a Nearl or a Baronite.

The morning glare highlighted the outlines of the man in front of her, the passers-by, the shop windows. There was a sharpness in the sights and sounds that made her want to suck them in like sweets. The little man was tugging at the loose strands of his beard. Amulets, ampoules, bottles and tablets, cures and remedies for all. Cecilia became distracted. The cloying, rancid smell of a huddled tenement reached her; voices heard from the street stopped her short. Snippets of conversation, glimpses of possibilities and wheretofores – so expanded was her horizon that she could only stand there and feel the vibrations pass through her. She felt herself triumphantly alive. The little man she had thought such a quiz was staring at a face on an advertising card. It was a clean-shaven face with thoughtful eyebrows and crisp wing collar. A chemical change was taking place in Cecilia. A man with funds enough to hold his head high. Cecilia's head felt very fragile, as though it were made of glass. The sweet poignancy of the man's unguarded sighs was brought to her by the hum of the street. Cecilia was sideswiped by what was taking place inside her.

'That's the beard of a Baronite, my friend,' she declared. The street, so quick with life, had slowed down. This was just as well as her legs had gone. In one fell swoop, she sank to her knees and landed in the pharmacy's alcove. She leaned her forehead against the delicious, cool enamel of the tiles.

'Are you all right, my dear?' said the little man.

He escorted her across Praed Street, into Irongate Wharf Road, and before he left her at the door of number 38, he tipped his bowler and bowed.

'That's a gentleman,' decided Cecilia, as she closed the door behind her. She turned round. She had made up her mind. Adelaide and Doris, her nieces, were sitting on the bed. It was a wretched, collapsed old thing made of wood and iron. Herbert had once joked that it looked as if it had been rescued from a fire, then used for a barricade and finally dug out of a dust heap to be carried home by George. The girls were tied together with an old rag. Emily-Maria was on her knees before the grate, scrubbing and explaining the situation.

It didn't quite happen as Cecilia had envisioned. On any other Monday, this would have been wash-day. Emily-Maria would have been washing clothes at the public baths to earn a few pennies. Emily-Elsie would have been minding her sisters and turning the mangle.

'Children crawling in the muck, with sticky, nasty hands and putting them in their mouths and crying. There's nowhere to put the tea things, and bugs, all these bugs. Tumbling up and down the stairs, day and night, they won't stay still, and the soot creeps everywhere, and I keep trying but I can't stop it. "You've met your Waterloo here." He can laugh. It's everywhere. Someone tell me where there is a room without dust, beetles, mice, cracks, filth, rot. It's like a game of draughts. One room to another . . . They're all the same.'

'What are you doing, Emily?' Cecilia bent over her sister.

'What are you doing, Emily?' Emily-Elsie was playing with a doll.

Sometimes Dolly would take me on walks up Streatham High Road. A toyshop attracted my attention and I pulled her inside. A bell rang as the door closed behind us, announcing our entry into a fairy grotto. This was the world I longed to inhabit in miniature. It was coloured in pristine pink and blue, various in its delights, and prettily packaged. I found theatres, costumes, eyes that sparkled like sapphires, cheeks that glistened with rouge, air stewardesses, princesses, stable girls, entire armies complete with cavalry, fireworks and round-bellied bears. It was rare that we left without Dolly making a purchase.

Emily-Elsie's doll was long and dangly like the one she had seen in a shop window – a figure of wire and wax mounted on a stand. This one was lying in Emily-Elsie's lap on a home-made bed. It had a gauzy frock. It was hard to keep warm. The wind was coming in through the casement in icy gusts blowing the rags that Mother had washed and hung on a line. They waved like flags in the air. The wind moaned down the chimney as well like a howling ghost. It was very dark because of all the chimneys of the other buildings that crushed together.

Emily-Maria had been out all day. The better set of person tried to earn a respectable living. Emily-Maria charred in a large white house near Regent's Park. The term 'char' originally meant 'a turn; time; occasion', with the relevant sense being 'a turn of household work'. It derives from Old English. There have always been chars, but they have not always been drudges. Emily-Maria put up with the housekeeper telling her the proper way to polish a grate, clean a mantelpiece or remove stains from papered walls for ½d a day. She was a charwoman, which by now meant that her work was considered a chore, a task marked by drudgery. However, her surroundings were respite from the room she helped to pay for. It was in a paved court with posts at each end to stop carriages coming in. The court had a gutter down the middle into which tenants emptied their privies. The gutter was a standing rivulet of waste and excrement. The stench made you gag. The water that came out of the standing pump was brown and brackish. Cholera and dysentery were rife. The front doors were always open, and Cecilia stumbled up the staircase with no handrail. The lower set of people were a miserable, shifty bunch. The man would be a gambler, sharper or thief and the woman would be on the streets. These were the pauper colonies; like rooks' nests, alive with grubs and flies, so close-knit as to be indistinguishable; families sleeping, living and dying together.

'What are you doing, Emily?'

'Clean and proper. You'll see.'

'Where's Daisy?'

'I know it's here somewhere he slinks out he thinks I don't know he smells of her and if it's not her it's another one I can't find her anywhere.'

Bone-picker, rag-gatherer, pure-finder, dredgerman, mudlark, sewer-hunter, night-soil man, a pause for breath, and in one last gush – bunter, tosher, and shoreman. Herbert amused himself by reeling off lists of possible jobs for George. It made Cecilia laugh. Laughing at others took her mind off her troubles, though she couldn't help feeling a twinge of guilt.

❊   ❊   ❊

My father wore a thick gold chain with lucky charms hanging from it. The pale blue eye, with a film over it and a black dot in the centre, was to ward off the envy of others. The red coral horn promised plenty. After his flying visit from Africa, I found a photograph he had left behind. It was a portrait of a smiling woman leaning towards the camera. She was wearing a low top and a gold chain with the *malocchio* and the *cornicello*.

George's worsted trousers, where they were not darned, were in holes, and his coat was shiny, which meant that the streets were his home. In his shabbiness, he was part of the crowd. Other seedy fellows nodded in silent recognition as he passed the Brazen Head on Bell Street – a mere beer shop – and kept on his way to Marylebone where he would have a taste of luxury before he lost it all. And so he passed the graceful mound of the station – more like a temple than a terminus – and picked up his feet to march more purposefully. Before he opened the door to the Great Central Hotel, he paused to adjust his coat and throw back his shoulders. He strode in, drew up an armchair to the empty fireplace and rested his feet on the fender as though warming them. A waiter appeared, and he gave his order: 'Brandy and water. Hot.'

'This is the lounge bar. It is for gentlemen who are staying in the hotel,' said the waiter.

George took his feet from the fender, and rising slowly, held the gaze of the startled waiter. He was a short man, and very thin, but there was a menace in his attitude that obliged the waiter to take a step backwards.

'Brandy and water. Hot. D'ye hear?'

George sat back down and waited.

*   *   *

Emily-Elsie had never been to an infirmary before so she did not know what to expect. In the female ward, she lay on a trestle on the floor with a straw mat under her head. Her hair had been shaved till she was bald. She was wearing a coarse hemp gown that made her skin chafe. There were around seventy other pauper girls lying in rows in the large hall. They were keening, shouting, moaning, screaming and coughing. Their cries were everything she had ever heard that had threatened to overwhelm the tune she played in her head with all the resolution of a marching band holding aloft a blood and fire flag. There was one high note that with particular precision cut through the cacophony of suffering. To her consternation, she heard that she was whining with pain and fear. The nurse appeared. She was an elderly, dishevelled woman who smelt like a pub in the Grove. She began her treatment of Emily-Elsie by shaking the girl upright. Then she gave her some physic from a bottle, having tasted it first herself.

The consequences of Herbert's scam came thick and fast. George Smith was admitted to the Salvation Army Shelter in Lisson Grove. Emily-Maria returned to her parents' one-room cottage in Ware. She took two of her four daughters with her. Herbert vowed to do something to help. But in the meantime, he still had the proceeds from the hoisted coal. So he bought himself and Cecilia third-class train tickets to Southend-on-Sea. He had a contact there. It was the place to go. Cecilia had never been on a train before. She had ideas as to what she would do when she alighted.

'Let me take Daisy,' she begged her sister, who had left the baby in the porch of St Mary's on Paddington Green. The baby who writhed and wriggled like an eel came back because Cecilia went to fetch her. There wasn't room at Ma and Pa's, so Daisy could go with Cecilia.

At the age of nine, Emily-Elsie Smith was sent from the workhouse to the St Marylebone Cripples' Home and Industrial School for Girls. So that was Emily-Elsie taken care of.

I thought I had found my happy hunting ground in Southall. But I needed a holiday from my nadir.

'D'yer hear about Killer?' Pete asked me. I shook my head. We were on the number 607 bus to Ealing Broadway. But there was a scene-of-crime tape cordoning off the road. 'Some dipstick Somali ripped off Sheneice. The idiot took her night's takings. Now Sheneice is Killer's daughter. So what does Killer do? He only goes and breaks a bottle and stabs the guy four times in the heart. Now the guy's dead and that's why the busies are stopping the traffic. Honestly,' he sighed.

Pete rarely left Southall. 'Only to fight the Irish,' he would grin. But when he did he acted the tour guide to this strange world outside his domain.

'You get on a bus. There's all these unfriendlies — you know they're not quite citizens yet. And then there's the young Muslims. You've got to watch them.'

'Why?'

'They're explosive.'

We might have been travelling on a bus full of masked subversives, or retributive descendants of the British Empire. Pete, the soldier protecting Her Majesty's possessions, found enemies everywhere. More than that, the passengers on the 607 TfL bus heightened the fear of being overwhelmed by otherness, so strange and potentially dangerous were these Bosnians, Somalis, Albanians, Afghans, Punjabi warriors, and Bengali tigers. These others. Pete was in defensive mode.

'On the whole, though, why should I leave?' he argued with no one in particular but so that everyone could hear him. He looked around him and took in the packed contents of the sausage-shaped container with a regal, six-foot-four sweep. He bent and swayed with the permutations of the bendy bus, like a willow tree dipping its branches into a fast current.

'Everywhere is on the way to Southall. You can get anything you want there. In the old days, I'd pick up an empty pack of cigarettes, walk up and down The Broadway asking people for tabs and I'd have a full deck in twenty minutes. Anyway, if you really have to go, the express trains come in fast through the station. And they don't stop. So that's one way out of Southall.'

Pete was nervous because I had decided to visit Freddie in Southend-on-Sea. He was not used to a woman leaving his orbit unless she was his mother. I was visiting Freddie because Pete's drugs weren't hard enough and they weren't coming fast enough.

The last time I had seen Freddie had been in a workshop at Her Majesty's pleasure. I went to the Kursaal on the eastern esplanade of Marine Parade, and what did I find? Another lanky frame in a silky sports ensemble bent over a pool table, deep in concentration. When he rose to consider who had entered the Dome, he paused the game, signalled to his partner, and stood upright. He didn't often achieve stillness so the fact that he did meant something. It was a sign. Freddie had eyes like grey pebbles. They were shrewd and screwed up when he thought; stony when considering. He was considering me now, and then he smiled. The still centre of his smile was enough for me. It was as though the world had stopped – or at least the whirring machinery on the seafront. Freddie's energy was different from the languid smoothness of Southall Pete. Southend Freddie had the fizz of bipolar madness about him. On the other hand, it could have been crack psychosis.

That night I woke up and realised something. I had worked in a men's prison in order to get closer to my father. In so doing, I ended up on a wild goose chase for more men like him. It's funny how things work out. Pretty Little Polly Perkins of Paddington Green ended her song, the milkman tells us, by marrying not a Wi-count, nor a Nearl, nor yet a Baronite, but a 'bow-legged bus conductor of a tuppenny bus'. Cecilia knew that the enchantment would have to wait for some other time. Herbert had done a vanishing trick. For now, she had her baby boy, Herbert – and Daisy.

Chapter Thirteen

ONE BRIGHT SPOT

Southend at night is ablaze with illuminations. Marine Parade, from Pier Hill to the Kursaal, is gaudy with gambling joints and public houses advertising nocturnal distractions. It is as though New York's Broadway had been transported to a seaside shanty town, and in the process lost some of its high-rise splendour. The flatness of Essex cannot be escaped, and the scent of dereliction on Marine Parade vies with that of hot dogs and candyfloss.

The lights of Southend will always blaze, but Freddie's show was a once-in-a-lifetime spectacular.

'We're bending light!' he shouted, hurling a Catherine wheel into the black depths of the fireplace. It was the most dazzling choreography of starbursts and flames, an electric storm reconfigured in emblazoned dots and languishing trails, a kaleidoscope let loose in a living room. For Freddie, it was an expedition into the black hole at the centre of Centaurus A, the one that promises to devour everything: hope, faith, ambitions, Stone Island crushed cotton jackets, Adidas chalk-white trainers, brown fields, housing estates, long silent avenues, stolen cars and the sea grey as Whistler's mother. It all vanished in a twinkle of Freddie's eye, because, when he wasn't conducting chemical experiments, he conjured galaxies in the Milky Way.

'This one's for you,' he smiled, as the last rocket kissed the velvet sky, and, because what passed between us would never come to fruition, I faded out. And then, because it could only go this way, the fire started.

She could taste the brine on her tongue. As she breathed in, the atmosphere felt so clean it was as though she were ventilating her lungs. And yet here she was climbing another broken staircase up to another rented room, a room like all the others, her sister would say: smeared, smutty, and smelling of disappointment. There was a layer, like the skin of boiled milk, of dust, ashes and grease over the walls and floorboards. Cecilia knew that no amount of scrubbing could wipe it off. She smiled and looked through the window. The room was on the first floor of number 2 in a small row of elderly brick and timber houses. One push and they'd tumble into the mud-flats they presided over. Number 2 Prospect Place, Southend-on-Sea, had been built as a fisherman's cottage in a previous century. Now it was rented, room by room, to Londoners escaping the city. She sat on a three-legged stool at a patched-up window overlooking a beach, her face sprayed by a silver mist.

'How refreshing!'

Cecilia had learned to find sustenance in thin air; in this sea shower; in the waves flooded with light, and in the children unused to playing on a beach, overseen by wardens. The pangs of hunger and fear had dimmed into the peace of acceptance. She contemplated the oysters contained in beds, and the nets of crabs past the bathing huts. She looked down at her work again. Her hands, busy in her lap, were small and well kept, although the skin was beginning to spot. She sighed. The vibrations of a bird beating its wings hovered in her ear, its cries mimicking those of open-mouthed babies. She was drawn once again to the waves' hoarse repetition, laying the foundations for a very particular education.

'Comfrey, rue, horehound.' She counted them off as she dropped them into the pot.

When she was a child, the first girl after four boys, she had trekked across golden fields of barley with her mother. She had climbed inside the brambles and branches of the oldest hedgerow in the county, in search of her mother's herbs.

'This one comes under the sign of the lion; Sol claims dominion over it.' She held up a weak and trailing branch of pale green leaves spotted with black. 'Taken while fasting, for pains in the head.'

The aroma bubbling out of the pot was dense and bitter. Daisy grimaced.

Daisy's favourite place in the world was Southend. A seaside resort so close to London, which was where her family came from, just two hours by the ferry from Tower Hill. Visitors to Southend called it Whitechapel-on-Sea. Daisy loved to watch them promenading along the longest pier in the world. It stretched all the way to the Isle of Sheppey. She fancied she could almost touch it. Aunt Cecilia and little Herbert laughed when she tried. She joined hands with Herbert and followed Cecilia back to the Greens that spread away from the seafront. They were tracking two types from London.

'Weedon,' she heard the lady say.

'He's a famous showman,' said her aunt Cecilia, 'who's brought his play here from London.' She pointed to posters on the walls that announced a forthcoming theatrical entertainment from Weedon Grossmith.

For now, Weedon was enjoying the Greens. Smooth lawns lit by gaslight, the Greens provided swings and round-abouts, shooting galleries, coconut shies and weighing machines. The Jolly Boys – Southend's comic duettists – were on that night. Weedon smiled at the gasps of amazement and laughter that hung in the air. But his young lady ('I don't think she's his wife,' mused Cecilia) had locked eyes with Daisy whose hint of a smile beckoned her to a place just past the parade, just yonder.

Here in the Rookery, the ground was uneven and the mist tinged with jade. It was like stepping into a tunnel built of wild iris and sea campion. Daisy led the way through bowers of cobnut and hazel. Herbert chuckled at the lady's bewilder-ment. The pin in her hat had worked itself loose and strands of her hair – damp and frizzy – had caught in the dipping branches. She felt like the Fairy Queen with Cobweb and Moth in attendance. When the high wall of foliage thick-ened, she had to snake her way through it. In the darkness, clammy leaves brushed her face, teasing her with glimpses of the stained-glass, grey-green estuary.

And then, 'Ready,' she heard Cobweb whisper. It was as though a stage curtain had been pulled aside. The twining foliage and boughs opened into a copse that contained a cathedral hush. Daisy and Herbert were creating their own show. The lady smoothed her hair away from her face and feeling a rustle amongst her skirts smoothed her pockets over her hips. Something was amiss.

'Where's my purse?' she heard herself say. But there was no answer.

Freddie had gone round to see his boy P to check if he could lay him on an ounce of gear. P only had an eighth, which he let Freddie take, but in lieu of the rest, he did have another, equally appealing chemical to hand. P had just taken possession of a large amount of MDMA crystal, and this is exactly what it looked like – a glinting, silvery-white crystal.

'I'll tell you the truth.' Freddie's long legs unfurled and he lay back as though on a sunbed. We were in his headquarters, the unused seating area behind the forgotten pool tables in the amber glow of the Kursaal. 'I was proper out of it on various other substances.'

This was easy to believe, and surprising he found it necessary to point it out.

'I didn't take much persuading to accept a lump – on credit – to take with me, along with the eighth. This thing . . . is meant to be . . . the Mutt's Nuts.'

On credit. After putting 10 pence each way on horses, acquiring useless possessions on the never-never was Great-aunt Dolly's favourite way of forestalling death. Each week a parcel arrived, and the next one might be the one that would change everything. But in the meantime, it didn't matter because payment was deferred. Addicts are always on the lookout for a touch: that fabled, something-for-nothing, get-away-with-it-while-you-can introductory offer before you do a runner. And it always comes like a punch in the stomach when it's payback time.

'So I'm plotted up in the toilets of Raquel's crushing and sniffing this MDMA off the toilet seat. I'm in there for some time and people outside are beginning to notice. Someone starts bangin' on the door asking if I've got anything for sale – how the fuck do they know what I'm doing? I open the door half expecting to be confronted by the management and the bouncers, seeing as I'm banned from there anyway. But instead there's three bods, all about eighteen years old. I chip a splinter off, pull the first one into the cubicle and give him a Rizla to bomb it. He's clean-cut and has a shirt and tie on.' Not for long, I thought.

Immersed in the long, slow burn of his attention, I felt safe. I needed this focus to stabilise my own – catapulted as I was, like a ball in a game of bagatelle, buffeted by obstacles on the board that sent me into the gutter. But these were the rules of the game. And the gutter took me back to the starting point, my childhood. Freddie sold drugs, kept guns in his house, and lived off his nerves. This was why I liked him. To say that he was vulnerable, given his capacity for violence, is to say that he lived in the state of bewilderment I had experienced as a child, never knowing what would happen next, having little choice but to run with it. Freddie lived off his nerves; and like me, he was born guilty. But he was one step ahead: he committed crimes, so he had something to be guilty about.

Southend. A composition of slate-grey stillness, a persistent silence and miles of mud-flats reaching towards the River Thames. And there are fishermen here, too, who come and go seemingly as they please, by day and by night, hauling in their catches.

'He has boys down at the beach, you know,' my father's third wife told me, 'picking tourists' pockets.' We were in the spare bedroom of my father's house in the Caribbean, and she was packing her bags. 'They bring the credit cards to him, and then he sells them. And at night' – her confession of my father's sins could not be discharged quickly enough – 'boats come in from Venezuela.' She lowered her voice. 'You know, Venezuela.' I looked blankly at her.

'Cocaine,' she said, and with that, she zipped up her suit-case, and was gone.

My father just smiled, and continued to percolate his perfect mid-morning cappuccino.

Freddie was a straight-up drug dealer who respected the Law and could be disarmingly rueful. 'They're doing their job,' he would say when the handcuffs went on. Pete, on the other hand, was scheming and shady; a criminal who dissembled but could not catch himself in the act. He was a friend who would steal your wallet then help you look for it, believing all the time he had not stolen it. Strange rumours and subtle murmurings had been disturbing the haze of my mind for some time. Even if they had not, my addiction had a roving eye and relentless appetite. Freddie was an archetypal Essex boy. Southend, the former manor of Prittlewell, was where he promenaded.

'We've got personal, but that's it. So we've now got to go to P's for the pick-up. But I've lost our car. I lost it by lending it to Bulgarian Bob, who I was banged up with. He got released from jail after me so I picked him up from the gate. He didn't really know me, or what I did, so when he came and plotted up with us he sort of forgot about time (and his wife) for a week. Then he needed to get home live-oh and borrowed the car. I forgot to tell him that there was a wheel clamp in the boot that we had got someone to take off when we were picking up a parcel previously. Bob got stopped by the police, and they found the clamp, plus the five shots of crack and smack that I'd given him (in trouble). He'd done me a proper favour when I got locked up in 2001.'

The mist lifted in the afternoon, the sun came out and so did the visitors.

'We will be as naughty as we have to be,' Cecilia told the children. They loved Pier Hill Fairground. It had swings, a hurdy-gurdy and steam roundabouts. The Roly-Poly Ride gave you seasickness without having to leave dry land. It was a strange sight to see the people in their fine clothes being tossed around by machinery and screaming. Besides this, there were fortune-tellers – mysterious ladies with large painted eyes. Cecilia had a crêpe rose for Daisy's copper hair, and in her case under the bed she kept a sailor's hat for Herbert. He was a sleek baby boy, brown and thin and inter-esting-looking, with a gentle, pleading expression to his eyes. He could turn down the corners of his mouth to look espe-cially sad when occasion demanded.

'That's enough now,' laughed Cecilia, and continued with Daisy's lesson.

'This is white horehound. See its woolly stem and the hairs on its leaves. The 'Gyptians called it bull's blood. It grows where the soil is dry and sandy.' Daisy listened. 'Use it fresh, because its power is lost in keeping.'

When Cecilia pinched and rouged them, Daisy's cheeks were rosy. But her skin clung to her bones.

'By hook or by crook, or as your father would say,' with a nod to Herbert, 'by fan, downy and dookin,' Cecilia said, 'we shall manage.'

They ate crabs from the nets that Cecilia boiled on the grate, onions, apples, watery broth and penny loaves. They paid the rent each week. They had tea and sugar and there was 10d from the last pack. Once this pack was finished, it would be dusk and too dark to sew. Cecilia and Daisy – such quick, nimble fingers she had! – sewed eyes on to the cards. Baby Herbert passed the hooks into the eyes. Cecilia and Daisy then sewed down the hooks and the card was complete.

Cecilia marvelled to see Daisy's fingers move so quickly that at times she seemed to be stitching without either needle or thread. Presently she stopped; and, with a pair of scissors that darted like a silverfish, she snipped through a spider-fine length of cotton. If she was lucky, Daisy would catch a glimpse later of Mademoiselle de Rosa's lady dancers or the Frappini trapeze artists slipping in and out of ropes and ladders, jumping from shoulder to shoulder and never falling, always laughing. So triumphant.

Next door was the Southchurch Beach Cripples' Home, where crippled children from London were on a fortnight's visit courtesy of the Ragged Union. They had picked the right spot, near the newly erected Kursaal. Cecilia opened the window so that Herbert and Daisy could see the poor children in crocodile formation shuffle down to the beach. Buckets and spades, castles in the shimmering sands. Daisy waved and blew kisses, and received smiles and laughter in return. Cecilia called her back to her work. There were four dozen hooks and eyes on each card, and a gross of cards to a pack.

'Shall we calculate the number of stitches for each pack?' Cecilia asked. 'No! We have no time for mental arithmetic!'

At night, if they could not sleep, she told them stories.

'Her mother was dead. She buried her. Afterwards she couldn't bear to stay in that place. She took to wandering. She slept in barns and under hedges. She lived on berries and nuts. Her hair clogged into clumps. Her clothes became greasy rags. She was as bony as a whisper. She came back to town. An old woman took pity on her . . . There was a fine house where the young man had been struck down with a strange affliction. Once it had been a happy place. Now, even the mice in the cellar wept. She herself was a crippled maid. The master of the house had proclaimed if any woman could make his son happy, she could have him. But she was only a crippled scullery maid.

'Like the children next door, dears. Yes, just like them.'

It had not taken Cecilia long to summarise the situation. Since that moment in Marylebone she had surprised herself at how quick she was off the mark. The wrought-iron balconies and Georgian slimness of the Royal Terrace were still graceful, but the dust had settled and turned into muck. Weedon Grossmith was staying at number 1, with a woman twenty years younger than himself. She was registered as his wife. Beneath the tea-lights, the gaiety, and the lazy laughter, those in possession of a rare sensitivity felt something sullen and dangerous. The Terrace's reputation was questionable. At number 2, several unrelated single women resided under the patronage of a widowed female and two male servants. The women were 'laundry maids'. Sometimes they came to visit Cecilia. These were the times that Daisy and Herbert watched the water boil on the grate and a bitter stench filled the room. Sometimes it was too late and Cecilia was called to number 2. It was on one of these occasions that Cecilia spotted them preparing for an excursion. It was High Season, and they were a handsome couple. She saw the man press notes into the girl's hand. She mutely folded them into her velvet purse. Cecilia was sorry for the girl who could see nothing but stage lights and Weedon, but she had to eat, too.

Away from the shining mud-flats, Southend is crowded: tourists, shop workers, catering staff, fairground workers, office workers, unemployed workers, gamblers, perverts, drifters and pensioners from every town in the county. People wander around, unrelated, purposeless, most of them looking vaguely sullen, unhealthy and hostile.

'This is a place where you can enjoy yourself,' sighed Freddie, stretching out like a spider in his web in the Kursaal. By the Dome it's known, Southend's Kursaal opened in 1901.

Freddie's boys drifted in and out of the Grand Entrance oblivious to the gracious dome through which sunlight decanted like sparkling champagne into the empty silver bowl of the foyer. These days, the Grand Entrance was permeated with loss. Posters on its stained-glass windows offered rooms for hire for funeral wakes. Defunct comedians staged last-chance shows in its run-down theatre. Job Seeking no-hopers picked up shots on giro day. Freddie's clientele could spot his boys a mile off. When they weren't doing business, they were exchanging monosyllables with mobile phones. Stylish as dancers, in the Kursaal's sepia stillness they were lost boys stuck on a stage set for Peter Pan.

''E said you gave 'im a score.'

'Nah.'

'Nah.'

Long silence.

'Less 'ave it right. You oh 'im a ton.'

Super-slim phone slipped back into Aquascutum pocket. Summary justice done.

The dance hall had a floor in polished oak parquet laid on springs. The hundred and twenty-foot-long arcade had shops to either side and was laid out to simulate a street in Cairo. This led to the zoological gardens where the wild animals were on display. 'One Bright Spot' was how the Kursaal was presented to the public. It is a German word, meaning 'cure hall; a public room in a spa where the sick go to recuperate and recover'. Even criminals came here to cool off and gather strength.

They conveyed their meaning less by words than by significant jerks of the head. As such, I had that familiar sinking
feeling to which I was addicted, that I was missing something, or worse, and this was when it got interesting, that I
was the object of their silent discussion. The paranoia
surrounding drug supply and distribution ensures that the
drugs do their undercover mission without you having to
ingest them. But in the safety of the Kursaal's resounding
emptiness, Freddie could expand.

'I'm plotted up at P's, just about to drop some acid (about
eight tabs), when Reg pulls up in a stolen Vauxhall Cavalier
(red).' He nods in my direction, as though it is my insistence
on details that he is obliging. 'So anyway, Reg asks if I wants
to get high and go joyriding.'

Freddie turned to check that I was keeping up. 'Reg as in
Reg the Veg,' he explained. 'He was in a coma once.

'The windscreen looks as though it has been driven
through a war zone. Not good. Proper bait in fact. The ride's
pretty uneventful, apart from at some garage. Even though
we've got three grand in cash, Reg still has to drive off without paying for the petrol. We're only going to burn the car
later, so no drama. But we've still got personal on us, and
we've still got to pick up, so we don't really need to be
attracting attention to ourselves. We look hot enough as it is.
So I'm breathing more easy when we get to the Westcliff
service station and turn off to go into town. We go to see if
we can locate and pick up Darren (crack-lovin' Romeo!) and
take him with us. He's worth the entertainment value alone.
Darren's dad works for Revenue & Customs, a proper straight
bod, good home and all that. But Darren? He's proper wild-
style, seriously funny.'

*   *   *

The Thames pours into the sea here, and each night the barges dock to take their load of dust. With two mates from Hertfordshire, George was employed on a barge called the *Progress*. They came from Millwall Docks along the river to the estuary at Essex. Later George would bring Emily-Maria and their younger daughters to live in the stable mews behind Royal Terrace. Sometimes they would send Emily-Elsie the fare for a day's return.

Sometimes it was too late for a potion. Cecilia brought her case out from under the bed, and sent Daisy and Herbert out to play. They were quiet children, 'meek and mild', she smiled, as the tearful laundry maid paused to pat the girl's curls. 'No one gets a peep out of her,' said Cecilia, as though with pride. The laundry maid was too absorbed in her own sorrow to comment. But on the bowling greens and open spaces of Southend-on-Sea, Daisy performed cartwheels while Herbert recited nursery rhymes:

'Then came the Most Holy, blessed be He, and slew the slaughterer who had slaughtered the ox which had drunk the water which had burnt the staff which had smitten the dog which had bitten the cat which had eaten the kid my father had bought for two zuzim; only one kid, only one kid.'

'The rabbis tell us that the cat is Babylon, the dog is Persia, the staff is Greece,' but those who stopped to admire the charming children rarely stayed to listen to the woman's strangeness.

Daisy took Herbert by the hand through the wooded walkway at Royal Terrace. Dense shrubberies and rock pools – a veritable forest – dropped down the side of the cliff and led the strolling pedestrians down to the seafront. The longest pier in the world took them far out to a shining sea beyond the oyster beds and barges.

'The old river god lives there,' Cecilia told them. 'He rises each night from the mud and the dust.' Like a huge shoulder of water, obstructing the sky and rolling towards them with irresistible beauty and force.

Daisy listened in the dark. The wind was roaring down the chimney as though, at any moment, it would burst into the room – enraged and storming like an angry man. She was enthralled and frightened and entirely used to it. The river god lived in Southend. Coming in from the west in the drear and sleet, the *Progress* navigated the great breadth of the estuary. The famous Thames barges sat in brown bunches like bruised fingers splayed upon the water. The sea-reach of the Thames was straight, and, once London was left behind, its banks were uninhabited. As George came into Southend, the land rose, shutting down his view with a wooded slope overgrown with bushes. When he spotted the low buildings on the eastern end of the shore, and the Dome sitting almost atop them, he knew he was in sight of Prospect Place. This was where Cecilia lived, in a house on the beach. Here, where the dust piles were. Cecilia laughed when she heard Southend's worthies complain about the stench that permeated the eastern stretches of Marine Parade. George imagined he could see her profile lit by a candle in the window. The sound of the waves suggested to him the time when he was drowning in brandy and water. George came to Southend converted to temperance. The Sally Army drummed it into him. 'Our shelter from the stormy blast, and our eternal home.' Hymns and sermons in exchange for soup and shut-eye. But George did not belong to the cohorts of scoffers. He was brought to his knees and he was raised again. He and his mates swept up the dust piles along the harbour of lost dreams.

*   *   *

Under cover of night is when real life is conducted. The conventional world is one of pretence, formalities and going through the motions. In a very real sense, it's a waste of time. Or, at the very least, a way of marking time.

It was late. The empty arms of the stationary rides of the Sea Life Adventure Theme Park reached out to a handful of dimly distant stars. Freddie was taking me on a run with Reg. As we piled into the stolen Cavalier, he was already separating the acid for distribution.

'These are extremely strong trips,' he warned. 'So thirty minutes from now we are going to be proper fucked.'

The main drag blurred past us in a neon streak of amusement arcades, and yet there was a distinct lack of soundtrack both inside and outside the car. Pleasure was being pursued with a steely-eyed focus. There was nothing to say, and nothing could be allowed to get in the way. Not even the car which was an easy-come-easy-go plaything to Reg, so he toyed with it; clipping other cars, doing skids, wheel spins, and racing all-comers. I rolled with the punches, but alarm mounted as a carload of boy racers took him on. This spurred Reg on. He had to show them that their recklessness was as nothing compared to his.

'They're getting worried,' Freddie laughed, when Reg started playing dodgem at 100 mph. The competition dropped out and didn't stop to complain about the scrapes to their car. When the car itself started protesting, Reg pulled up in the forecourt of a Little Chef. It wasn't a comfort break. While I was emptying the contents of my stomach, Savva was dousing the car with a can of petrol he had thoughtfully placed in the boot. He ragged the tank and set it alight.

Cars do not blow up as they do on television.

'Nah,' Reg explained. 'To get them to go pop you have to fill the inside with petrol, close the doors and windows and have a full tank to start with.'

The Cavalier lifted twelve inches off the ground before burning steadily. We sat in the bus shelter across the road, watching smoke and fire engulf metal.

'No prints. No evidence,' said Reg. Sirens started.

'Now we want to get to Westcliff live-oh.'

Freddie was planning to burgle a newsagent's in the vicinity. He had been right about the trip. But the Technicolor precision, wide-angled vision and wraparound sound did not stop me rehearsing my performance in the dock. Kidnap; coercion; helpless female; look at the size of him; he held a gun to my head! (that comes later): very well, I did know what I was doing but I couldn't stop myself. We walked in silence but all I could hear was a confusion of pleas and persecutory voices: yes, I admit it. It was my fault. You've been here before. Yes, but I've run out of . . . excuses? And so on, along the broad front of Westcliff. On a road of semis, away from the gleaming black seafront and the burning Cavalier, Reg made his choice: a ('nearly new') Ford Escort — 'easy access'. He Stillsoned the ignition, broke the steering lock, and we were in.

'This appears to be owned by some Asian feller,' Freddie remarked, taking in the religious mobiles on the dashboard. He opened the back door for me, and a blue mask and red tongue flew into my face. I was in the back seat of a stolen Ford Escort adorned with Hindu deities. Auntie's oily black hair slicked back in a bun returned to smother me. Her forehead punctuated with a dot creased into a smile as she opened the till to receive my payment. Smiling to smooth over my puzzlement at the sickening fragrance floating from her back

room and saturating her shop. It reminded me of my childhood. She sat there nodding. A scent like this, you never
forget. It clings to you. Like a miasma, it seems to bring
contagion with it, and I knew I had drunk it in before.
Where? I wanted to ask. What is it? Cameford Court, on the
other side of the block, where Uncle James lived in a bare
and dirty flat that intrigued me. It was a shooting gallery
where veins were the bull's-eye. My Wicked Uncle as he
liked me to call him, was cooking and serving up heroin in
what looked like a laboratory. I wanted to stay and play, but
he sent me back to Mother's bitter loneliness. The blue
goddess rushed up at me and poked her tongue out.

'The Hindus have a goddess of destruction.' Freddie was
remembering his laminated certificate in Diversity Awareness
Training from Chelmsford Prison.

'Kali,' I burped, trying to stay conscious and heaving with
seasickness. ('Carly?' a voice in my head was goading and
tormenting me.)

'Well,' Freddie sniffed, 'I would certainly associate this
odour with Asians.'

Reg awaited instructions at the wheel. I lunged for air as
though I'd been immersed in churning waters. Reg was
twisting and writhing, white as ash, and Freddie handed me
a downer from a blister pack.

'DFs, otherwise known as DF118 dehydrocodeine. Made
by the experts. So you can trust them.'

Reg was rifling through documents in the glove compart-
ment.

'It is some Asian geezer's,' he confirmed.

'No drama,' Freddie said. 'Less jack it anyway.'

We were proper fucked.

Chapter Fourteen

'A COCKNEY'S LIFE FOR ME'

It was a lot of work but Cecilia and her youngsters were learning the art of invisibility. Weedon was dressed as though for dinner at the Savoy, silver-tipped walking stick, Gieves & Hawkes stripes, and brogues as bright as ebony. Despite the silk and feathers she had procured, it was clear that his lady friend felt awkward beside him. Daisy had a knack for making people feel comfortable. So she put herself forward. A dainty cherub with pinkish-red hair and blue eyes smiled at the lady. 'Annie.' Weedon tugged her arm in an effort to draw her attention back to himself. But Annie was hooked. She had seen this pretty child what seemed just a few moments ago – in the Grand Entrance to the Kursaal. She had mistaken the woman with her for a fortune-teller. But Cecilia had no crystal ball, just a pale-as-paper face and a steadfast gaze. The arcade, draped with magic lanterns and Turkish rugs, was packed with patterers and sand-dancers. The mingled scents of spices, oranges and beers were intoxicating; the jostling crowd almost hushed in the anticipation of delight. Weedon's voice rang out as he read the Bill of Fare:

'"Distorting Mirrors, a Trotting Track and Mysterious Caves: all this and more at the People's Palace. A great and permanent source of enjoyment to the toiling masses of the City of London."'

At the Café Chantant, Daisy and Herbert hung back as Weedon and Annie watched the Zulu warriors singing and dancing. These were real black men from the docks at Millwall, done up in grass skirts and feather caps, rolling their red eyes at the audience. Weedon laughed as Annie's grip on his arm tightened. There was more to come. Stretched taller and thinner, Annie saw a skeleton beside her. In the next moment, her blooming face burst into overripeness. She slid from his side and he had to push through the throngs to find her. Herbert and Daisy caught up with them in the zoological gardens where the lady was sitting under an artificial bower. Weedon was singing his brother's song, 'A Cockney's Life for Me', raising a crowd and making the lady blush again. He picked her a silk flower.

'Motherwort. A brown stalk, three or four foot high, spreading into many branches with leaves a sad green colour.'

'You know,' Cecilia heard Annie say, 'if a couple first catch sight of each other in a mirror, they will have a happy marriage.'

Weedon sighed.

'To see your reflection in a mirror is to see your own soul,' said Cecilia as she emerged from the Caves.

Here they were again, by the Trotting Track, the girl holding hands with the boy, still smiling. The child's hair was neatly arranged with a faded flower. Daisy was attired in worn black worsted. Herbert was following the lady's eyes and took his cue. The little boy, so thin, toddled up to the lady. Daisy came scurrying after. Before she knew it, she was surrounded – ring a ring of roses – they twirled around her, laughing.

'Come away, dears.' The woman smiled at her. Annie, in her confusion, was struck by her poise. She was nearly Weedon's age, but she had the look of a woman who had willingly acquiesced in the act of growing old. Weedon talked some more to his admirers, and the child opened her hand as though to wave. There was a leaf cupped in her palm.

'I will go on to the pier, Weedon. It's close to lodgings, and I am tired.'

'I done a paper round (for about a week) at this newsagent's when I was a little kid, so I know where the internal alarm system is. We just smash it on entry.'

During the day Freddie had already sprayed a couple of the sensors in the shop with photography-fixing spray, 'rendering them inoperable'.

'This should be easy. You stay in the car.'

Whereas I was on a downer, Freddie and Reg had decided to level out the confusion of the acid with the coolness of amphetamine.

'Speed makes you serious,' Freddie explained. 'We're a bit hyper, but that's a good thing as we need to finish this as soon as possible.'

It took several trips to take what they wanted. But Freddie and Reg, with all the unhurried, practised ease of removal men, loaded the car with boxes. 'We've cleared all the cigarettes, and a small float that was there. Plus a crate of family-pack fireworks.'

It was time for some rest and recreation.

Reg's mum's house was detached and his nearest neighbours were easy-going, so it was, 'The perfect place to take drugs. Especially when she isn't there.' Reg's mum was 'an old hippy' and her living room had a Glastonbury feel to it.

The walls were adorned with bare tree branches and dream-catchers. The paintwork was tinged with smoke from the deep-set inglenook fireplace and a collection of bongs.

There is nothing so comfortable as being numb. But obtaining the ingredients for numbness requires much effort and ingenuity, not to mention law-breaking. Then there is the skill involved in combining them. It is an expertise that takes extensive research to perfect. Reg was building a fire as we dropped the rest of the acid and dashed speed into glasses of ouzo. With the lights off and just the warm fire flickering in the slate hearth, the room lit up in a brilliant flare and simmered back down to a glow. For one long, pastoral moment, we sat stupefied, our goal achieved, until the most recent intake of drugs took effect. A wave of exhilaration took hold of both Freddie and Reg. For me, this wave of fresh energy converted into anxiety. I was fixed to the spot with fear.

The fireworks were retrieved from the car, which although stolen and used in a burglary still hadn't been dumped and burned. A suitable tape of looped and frantic beats per minute was played at full volume. A traffic light was the first to explode into the inglenook. A sparkling jet of green, amber and red raced around a pitch-black room.

'It doesn't just look good, it sort of feels good too,' Freddie hazarded. Soon, repeater shells, rocket cones and Roman candles were popping and whizzing with dizzying cascades of colour. As enthusiasm mounted, anything became fair game. Reg launched a jack-in-the-box on to the fire. Designed to smoulder for a few agonising instants and then suddenly to fire plumes of brightness into the air, it shot into the room like a bolt of lightning, leaving white tails behind it.

'This is seriously entertaining,' Freddie decided.

*   *   *

'So now we're all messed up on the Persians,' he was telling his boys the next day. Back in the Kursaal, his nylon zip-up still smouldering, 'with fireworks exploding, and no one really bothered'.

This was not strictly true. Inundated by shooting stars, grand juries, revelations, speed, DFs and ouzo, I had lost consciousness.

'Anyway, me and Reg was just in awe at the light show going on around us,' Freddie continued. 'At some point I became aware that the curtains were alight. I only just managed to stop Reg dashing a large glass of ouzo over them. Despite the severity of the situation we was laughing hysterically. As soon as the curtains was extinguished we resumed the night's activities. We started breaking open as many of the fireworks as we could and packing all the flammables into a plastic container. Once this was proper rammo with powder we splashed a bit of petrol on top and taped it up. Living one side of Reg's mum is P. On the other side, there's two or three fellas in their early twenties. They owe P some money, so when he popped his head over the garden wall, and saw what we was up to, he jumped in. We cut a hole in the container and pushed a rocket in. The size of this thing was beginning to make us a bit dairy. It's Reg's mum's neighbours, after all. But by now Darren's turned up and the command of the operation changes hands to a man who answers to no one. Sweet. Let Darren do it.

'Darren, the natural-born leader and anarchist, takes the homemade bomb (because that's what it is), breaks into the house next door, sets it in their garden, lights it, and makes his escape. The noise level from our side has dropped to zero. We're waiting for the snap, crackle and pop to begin. Nothing. Then Darren crashes through the front door just as the rocket (which doesn't explode as soon as you light it) pops and sets the whole thing off. It wasn't so much of a bang as more of a whoosh. The whole rear of the house was lit up and the neighbours' garden was instantly set ablaze.

'The place was burning like Hell. With an orange, green and pink twist. P and Darren scarpered. Me and Reg come to our senses, attached the hose to the tap in the kitchen and started spraying the neighbours' fencing. Them boys was out of bed in a flash – a massive, multicoloured flash. They, along with us, was trying desperately to battle the flames. What a joke. Even Guy Fawkes would have been proud of this turn-out,' he concluded.

I had fainted ('Lightweight!' Freddie teased) but the fire brought me round. Reg's mum's neighbours' house was burning like Hell.

That season, the same year my mother was born, the South-end Corporation Electricity Department staged an exhibition. It was a hot summer night. The main feature was the magic light show. The purpose of the exhibition was to demon-strate the latest in electrical domestic appliances, displayed in an all-electric flat.

All night, it seemed, they raised their voices in a chorus of despair. To hear them would drive a person mad. They wailed and shrieked for mercy ('Stop rattling my cage!' Pete demanded back in Southall) but deliverance was a long time coming. The enclosure housed cages containing five hundred monkeys from India and South America, a baby leopard trained by Monsieur Fernando of Paris, nine tigers, two Burmese elephants, a puma, a Tasmanian devil, a baby alliga-tor, squirrels, an opossum, a herd of Sudanese sheep, a fighting ram, a wallaby, ostriches, a lion and a lioness, wolves, eagles and a Civet cat. Only the Civet cat survived.

Over one thousand lamps and two miles of wiring had been utilised in a show that was considered a modern miracle. That night, the Kursaal burned like Hell. The animals were soon replaced. The show goes on. The Kursaal is a bowling alley now.

Something had happened to George. Daisy nodded and pointed to the walls. The two rooms in the stable mews were bare, except for the pages of the Bible that he had pasted from floor to ceiling. 'Pray for us your servants to the Lord your God, to save us from death; for we have added to all our other sins the great wickedness of . . .'

Emily-Elsie had got off the train at Southend-on-Sea for her monthly visit. But this time she was visibly pregnant. It was luck she got a day-return. No more Southend for Emily-Elsie.

Like a bad penny Herbert Senior turned up just as suddenly as he had disappeared. Soon he had Daisy dressed in black from head to toe. Cecilia sighed as she wrote a letter to her niece in London. 'Herbert is up to his tricks again.' But there were redeeming features. He took a new, larger room for them in a modern house with a shared indoor toilet. Herbert had moved up a level. 'He is now a *fakir*, and sometimes a count from Paris,' Cecilia wrote. She quoted the letters he crafted, including the careful copperplate and verbal bouquets: ' "Ma chère Madame! . . . I see from afar . . . a blushing rose . . . at pier's end." He comes and goes, Em, but I pay no mind.' It was of little note to Cecilia. Time was pressing in, and there was much to do.

Chapter Fifteen

WHO AM I?

In August, the large masses of rowan berries, which had been attracting admirers all summer, took on a velvety crimson hue. Nancy and I were strolling across Bixley Fields, discussing men. She shook her head when I mentioned Pete's name, and refused to discuss him. I longed to know what she hinted she knew but Nancy's resolve was unmovable. I showed her my family tree which was now growing roots that were deep and knotty. I had found Daniel Kingham's grandfather. In examining the documents that recorded his movements, I had traced his birth to Hertfordshire, on the Grand Union Canal, and then his position as a servant in Barnet, which did not last long before he made his way down Watling Street to London. Here he found a room in White Lion Passage, which curved like a dog's leg around the back of Turnham's Grand Concert Hall on what is now Edgware Road. This former public house, dating from the sixteenth century, became the Metropolitan Music Hall in 1864. It features in the 1950 film *The Blue Lamp*. The passage where Daniel lived is glimpsed as slimy as a snake. Dirk Bogarde's spiv slithers down it, en route to shooting a policeman. The Metropolitan Music Hall is now Paddington Green Police

Station, famous for the detention of terrorist suspects in its underground cells.

Under the arch to the entrance of Turnham's Grand Concert Hall, high brick walls rose steeply on either side of a cobbled interior street that branched into White Lion Place – a grand name for such a squalid courtyard – before curving sharply and exiting on to Harrow Road. On his right, Daniel had a rolling Roman road leading him to Paddington Green, and opposite him, Irongate Wharf Road, which led to the Basin of the Grand Union Canal and Paddington Station. 'In 1845' – I could barely contain my excitement as I showed Nancy the marriage certificate – 'Daniel, who worked as a carman, married a girl he met in a concert hall.'

She shrugged.

'You have to get a bilge pump,' she insisted. *Adam Bonny*'s sharp descent was inescapable but I could be as stubborn as Nancy. I pointed out the meadow vetchling with tongues of lilac and yellow, the creeping buttercup, the buzz of foraging flies and the bumble-bees. I was not coping with the demands of daily life and instead of facing my boat's nose dive, I was hoping the next drink or drug would fix it. I was convinced I would find a message in the next bottle or in the next branch of my family tree. Nancy had no choice but to abandon ship. She had made a new friend.

Betty was a barge-dweller from Bulls Bridge, by the 24-hour Tesco. Her family had been bargees going back generations. Her grandmother had queued every morning for a handout at the gates of Monsted's factory by the dock: 'for a pound of marge and a quart of tea'.

'I woke up each morning not knowing what mood my nan would be in. It was always a gamble.' Betty was broad and squat. Almost to emphasise her size and shape, she had shaved her eyebrows and head till they were bald. She was sitting in the middle of the field as we approached her, and initially I felt alarm at the sight of her, and then pity as I realised this woman would always cause people to readjust their expectations. Betty wore a heavy black kaftan and a black fantail hat. I wondered at the closeness she had mustered with Nancy. But most of all, I saw Nancy paying homage to the despair in which I was floundering, most frightening in her savage reinvention of herself. Nancy and I took our places, and she grunted her greeting. We fell into a respectful silence, and again, my friend's exquisite manners impressed themselves upon me. She waited for Betty to pass the joint. We were sitting in a circle on a blanket, surrounded by broken-down caravans, tall reeds and nettles. We passed a bottle of cider and the joint to and fro, and talked about the drug problem on Shackleton Estate. We were smoking skunk — the crack-head's default when crack is unavailable. Skunk propelled me into psychosis more times than I care to mention. But the psychosis had levelled out into an eerie numbness that encircled me. Nothing seemed quite real, least of all me. I smoked the skunk knowing I didn't want it. But what else was there to do? I'd deal with the consequences later.

'Instant gratification,' I sighed. 'That's why they do it.'

'They're slaves to their addictions,' said Betty. She was the kind of conversationalist who always has the last word, and so she pulled out her trump card.

'I had a friend who lost his arm from injecting. Then he nearly lost his other arm. It didn't happen. Fine. Finally, the doctors told him they'd have to amputate both legs. You know what he thought? "Good. They'll have to give me a motorised wheelchair: I'll be more mobile and I'll get more benefits." That's how they think. That's addicts for you.'

I was horrified for more reasons than I cared to admit.

'She's very strange,' Nancy admitted. 'But she gives me money and she makes me laugh.'

Chapter Sixteen

LIFE IN THE FAST LANE

I have a riddle for you.

Most Londoners don't realise that behind the railway stations the buzz and bustle stops. It's most discouraging to a man. All he could see were lines of track and rusting wagons. There was black sleet on the ground and a few feet above yellow fog hung like a blindfold waiting to be tied. Thick clay pipes were lying in a pile at his feet. The gaffer said to him, 'Shift those pipes, will you?' He was a house painter, a plumber's mate, and sometimes fancied himself a master builder. He didn't trouble himself to respond.

All along the dock, and in my boat, I felt the winds of autumn gathering strength. Berries were dropping thick and fast. 'This means a harsh winter,' said *Bob-A-Buoy*. He pointed out the rowan tree. 'You can brew a liquor from these berries: the Welsh call it Quickbeam.' Against the rising tide of night, with *Tempest* tugging at her moorings, Nancy and I stoked the stove. We worked in silence. I was trying to prise her away from Betty May's dark orbit with promises of Quickbeam's powers of revelation. The lights of the factory illuminated the pool of the canal and the row of demijohns on *Tempest*'s prow. We poured boiling water on top of crushed berries, sugar, yeast and citric acid.

The rowan tree has a five-pronged star as its flower. 'It's a pentagram.' *Bob-A-Buoy*, when I allowed him, loved to instruct. On the whole, his interruptions were welcome since he had made it his business to study the canal, its fruits and people. I liked his closeness to underground movements, and his gracious acceptance of fate. Living in a cabin six foot high had caused his back to curve in a permanent stoop. 'The boat won,' he smiled.

Nancy looked up from her labours.

'That's awful!' she cried. And I, too, got ready to lament. *Bob-A-Buoy* laughed.

'But the rowan's message is not to give up: hold on strong to the life force.' On occasion, if it suited me, I would listen to him. I find it very hard to listen.

In the darkness, I heard Nancy muttering darkly about the malign influence of her homicidal stepmother. We dipped our mugs into the brew. Nancy felt in need of the pentagram's protection. I would do anything for a drink. So we awaited the results of our concoction.

I am the face that peers through the leaves
I am the fear in a child's mind
Who am I?

This was the real world, where men knew what it was to beg and borrow a shilling to pay the rent when Friday came. The houses here were old and grey and falling down like drunkards. In a row, leaning on each other, with thin walls separating them so you were nearly in your neighbour's, and it was always dusty except when rain fell and then it was muddy. At the bottom of the street there was a dairy and he would swear to you with his hand on his heart that the cow had more room than them all. Just off Edgware Road and behind Baker Street, you would never believe that it was there – the slime, the patches, and rags. This was home.

Edgware Road was like a magnet. It represented the beginning and the end of the world. Every time he went there, it was the first time. He would never leave it and yet he could not stay still. He had the same feeling I had when, as a little girl, I drank Coca-Cola straight from the bottle, all in a rush. A million flashing lights, stars in the sky, laughter from wide-open doors, red velvet saloon bars, huge posters, rich people, music halls and buses and carts, and Daniel Alfred Kingham, like the first Daniel, wearing his straw hat in the city of London.

My great-grandfather was a member of the Radical Working Men's Club on Paddington Green.

Dance now:
I am born on May Morning – by sticks, bells, and ribbons
I am the dancer – with his six fools

His father, like Emily-Elsie, was from St Mary-le-Bon.

I am the old grain – sown with the seed
I am the flame – in the pumpkin's grin
I am the spirit – in the kern-baby's bosom

His grandfather was also called Daniel Kingham. This was his mark.

I felt close to something that night on *Tempest* – I could see it, darting through the bushes, flitting like a shadow, to Bixley Fields beyond.

It was 1845 and Turnham's Grand Concert Hall was setting a trend that would be copied all over London. Every night there was a concert, admittance tuppence. The doors swung open and the surge of excitement started in the pit of Daniel's stomach. The atmosphere wrapped him in its warmth – engaging all his senses, and filling his frame with a delicious hunger and the glowing certainty that this was the place to feed it. The stage was set on tiers of boxes, and a tapestry cloth was pulled back to reveal a girl who had the same name as his mother. Miss Eliza of Harrow Road had watery blue eyes like ink that has been washed from the page. The fire had already burned out of her but she warbled charmingly to an organ accompaniment. Soon after their marriage at St Mary's on Paddington Green she dropped dead outside the Bazaar on Baker Street. Aged twenty-four, she died of 'natural causes'. At the age of twenty-five, Daniel, the first Kingham to reach London, was a widower.

Chapter Seventeen

PIRATES OF THE CARIBBEAN

This time he was not alone. A young woman and a little girl stood either side of him. My father was in his sixties. He was still slim with long, elegant limbs in Yves St Laurent shorts, a crocodile-skin belt, matching shoes, and a silk shirt. He introduced me to his wife, Ana Sol, from the Dominican Rebublic. She was twenty-one. Their daughter, Sasha, was six. I did a quick calculation and found the result disturbing. The warmth of the night sky smoothed over my awkwardness and I did what seemed expedient: I looked pleased to meet them. That morning, on 1 April 1995, I had boarded a plane at Heathrow Airport for Sint Maarten in the Netherlands Antilles. I was not sure what to expect. I had not seen my father for ten years. All I knew was that he was running a large casino in a tourist resort on Maho Bay. The 747 landed on the narrow runway of Princess Juliana Airport and I felt as though I were walking into a Graham Greene novel.

'The beach backed on to scrubland,' I told Pete, 'and there was a shack where they were serving drinks. The French side is prettier than the Dutch, less cultivated.'

'Mmm,' he said, hunched over the frayed green baize. Pete had a laissez-faire attitude towards our relationship. The first flush of romance had lasted the length of a session before rapid appraisals set in. It was good to have me around, because I had 'a touch of class'; but if I wasn't around, it didn't really matter. As for me, he was my supplier – of drugs, the inside track, and eternal youth. I could not take him seriously so I did not have to admit I was getting older. Most of all, I did not want to take myself seriously because that might involve some effort. And so I stole from myself all the opportunities my parents and those who came before them had worked so hard for.

'I met a woman, and she pointed to a boat anchored in the bay – a schooner with two wooden masts and white sails. It looked like a pirate's ship.'

'All right, Echoe. What's up?' A street urchin, naked under her off-white negligee, had burst through the doorway of the Brickmakers'. Her face was creased into dark, melancholy furrows making her look far older than her childish frame. She was wringing her hands and sobbing. Pete bundled this distraught girl-woman into the Ladies'. None of the turbaned punters raised an eyebrow. They continued to sit in silence at the bar, contemplating bottles of Cobra with weary brown eyes that had seen everything. Pete's sidekick at the pool table, Gabriel, was oversedated on Tramadol and Subutex. He was slumped in his seat, grateful for a break from the game. It was as though only I had seen this apparition.

I am the lost soul – under the misericord
I am the oak – against the stars

'Go on, honey, I'm listening,' Pete said, back from the Ladies' and pulling Gabriel into an upright position.

'She bought me another mudslinger and we swam out to the boat.'

'Mine's a brandy and Coke,' announced Sheena, ready to do business with raped sex workers, Southall Sisters, and abusive Beemer Boys if necessary. But only when she had had a fortifying drink – preferably one that lasted all night. I had watched Sheena through the smeared panes of the gabled window, waiting for the moment to make her entrance. When she walked into a room, she wanted the atmosphere to change.

'All right, She?' Gabriel jerked his chin up from his chest. Even though he was standing, balanced by his pool cue, he had managed to fall asleep.

Sheena was thirty-eight years old, and bargained on the fact that she was imposing. Before she had started smoking crack and heroin, she had weighed eighteen stone, and been the terror of Southall. Now that she was on three bags a day, she was down to eleven stone. She considered this to be 'a result'. But a diet of crack, heroin and Turkey Twizzlers leaves the skin grey and knotty. So she had to do a lot of bargaining. And she hadn't lost her passion for food so, although she was banned from Marks & Spencer, Sainsbury's and Tesco, there was still Iceland to plunder. (Nature's Bounty – I thought I had found it beside the canal.) The trouble for Sheena was that she didn't have a microwave, and using the oven was a manoeuvre too far. So, before her shift on Orchard Street, Sheena serviced the staff of Crunchy Chicken. In part-payment for her favours, she received a family-sized basket of nuggets and chips.

Her phone rang. She checked to see who it was, and started crying in preparation for what was to come. Her four children, ranging from café au lait to speckledy hen, had been taken from her some years previously. Since their fathers had

long since gone, they lived in a foster home. After a few
monosyllables and a series of justifications, she came off the
phone. She was sobbing. She had forgotten her son's birth-
day. Her wails grew louder, a knee-jerk response to
intimations of guilt. When she had finished, I asked her how
her children were.

'I'm OK,' she sniffed, which summed it up. Ten minutes
later, a brandy and Coke had taken her mind off her broken
family. Like me, she elaborated on the theme from a distance.

'Listen to this, right, eez got 'is 'ands on a shitload of snide
trainers . . . right. And Sheneice, right, I saw her down
Ealing, on the dip, like. Using the baby as a smother, like.
They'll take it off 'er if she's not careful.' A pause while she
remembered her own babies. 'I tell you what, right, for them
two a wide-screen's something you sell to get an eighth. You
should see their gaff. There's nuffink in it. No fridge, no
cooker, no shelves. They've stripped it all dahn and sold it!'
Only when she had reached the point where there was nothing more to sell, do or say, could she stop.

'The water was so clear and light it was like swimming
through a slipstream. I could hear the ship's rigging creak as
we neared it. But it kept disappearing behind the next wave.
My arms were sawing and I was beginning to feel I couldn't
go any further. Then she turned to me . . .'

'Is it your round?' Sheena wanted another before she
barged into the toilet to 'sort' Echoe.

'. . . She was just ahead of me, and she said, "We're nearly
there."'

The dense, clammy heat, and arriving at night at a small island
airport, reminded me of a flight to Freeport in Grand Bahama
that I had taken with my mother when I was eight. At that

point, I had not seen my father for a year or so. The alternating years of his absences and presences compress and elongate like a string wrapped round a yo-yo. But I remember my father waiting for me – his eyes like black searchlights meeting my own. I ran across the runway into his arms. He laughed and embraced me. In that moment, certain of my father's attention, I had it all. But then, just as quickly, I lost it.

Ana Sol was black with a Hispanic influence, gracious in a stiff, boutique version of Antillean style. But her youth did not carry the grande-dame manner well. Her severity dwindled into petulance. None of us spoke. I sat next to my honey-toned half-sister. She had inherited her mother's curling eyelashes, spun-sugar hair and self-conscious prettiness. The buzz of the air conditioning supported our silence. In the darkness I saw we were on a ring road that ran parallel to a clean strip of beach. The shops lined the road like a barrier to the sea's invitation. Dutch Sint Maarten, I could see, had lost its wilderness.

I scanned the pit, looking for my father. American tourists were crowded round the tables. Croupiers officiated in black dinner suits. Away from the floor, flanked by shift bosses, was my father. He introduced me to two unmistakably southern, swarthy Italians who did not smile at the introduction. Three men were playing poker at the high-rollers' table. They were young with glossy black curls and olive skin. They were too slim and poised to be Americans, and they spoke in Spanish monosyllables. I guessed they were Venezuelan.

'The Venezuelans bring the drugs in,' Ana Sol told me. 'The drugs come in on boats at night.'

'Last night he held a gun to a man's head.'

Freddie liked to tell the story of how he was once woken in the middle of the night by a friend wielding a knife.

Freddie's friend forced him at knifepoint to the place where he knew Freddie buried his stash. He then watched as Freddie dug in the undergrowth of his neighbour's garden. Then came Freddie's masterstroke. This particular Tupperware container contained a gun.

My father walked up to his wife's lover in the middle of the dance floor of a nightclub on the French side and held a gun to the man's head. The police were called. My father handed the gun to his 'private detective', who was subsequently taken into custody. The 'detective' was a small brown man who came to my father's house each day to be spoken to privately.

'They'll release him without charge,' my father assured me, and they did. On the Dutch side, my father had some pull. I asked him who owned the casino.

'Two Sicilians,' was his reply.

'I've known a few of those international types,' Pete said. 'I used to do business in Brixton.'

Pete learnt his trade in the Army. The most important lesson of all was how to keep a poker face. In Belfast, he was spat at and abused every day. He learnt not to react to provocation. At Enniskillen he picked up body parts and bagged them for identification. He had learnt not to react.

'Those Sicilians are playing on my mind.'

'It's intriguing, honey,' Pete agreed. He left the Army when they introduced random drug tests. Smoking several skunk joints a day helped him not to react. But sometimes, skunk isn't enough, just as, after a while, alcohol fails to deliver. This is when reinforcements are needed, and they are called upon usually at three o'clock in the morning, when the Shackleton Estate is brimming with silence, and there are so many horrors only white can blot them out.

Crack works by increasing the effects of dopamine and serotonin so that the elevation achieved from blazing rocks irradiates the brain. But if you go 'bang at it', as Pete and Sheena did, it soon leads to a dramatic depletion of feel-good transmitters and thus the inevitable crash. This heralds the first of many, since the central nervous system becomes desensitised, the highs get lower and lower, and the cravings more intense. Pete was left chasing that radiant feeling as though he were on a 007 mission. Soon, he was on the filthy floor of his bedroom, crawling on his hands and knees looking for that last piece of rock that had fallen out of the pipe and was still burning a hole in the carpet. It was still there, if only he could find it.

I, too, was on a mission.

'So I looked these two Sicilians up. One of them was arrested a few years back on charges of money laundering, and he was charged with being part of a criminal organisation.'

'No surprises there, then.'

'According to the Italian police, my father works for Caribbean partners in a ring that buys real estate with Cosa Nostra money. They also do business with the financier of Osama bin Laden.'

'Get Miss Marple!' Pete barked, and licked his lips dry with anxiety.

'One of them is in prison for blowing up a judge. It's just like in the 1960s when Meyer Lansky was doing Mob business in Cuba.'

The searchlight was safely focused on a remote time and place. Pete continued stalking the table with his pool cue, propping up a nodding Gabriel, and assumed a knowing air.

'Meyer Lansky is the Jewish mobster in *The Godfather*. The one they call Hyman Roth.'

'Which *Godfather*?' he asked, in case I was bluffing him.

'*Two.*'

'He swims with the fishes?'

'I think that's *One*. Anyway, an integral part of this system was a casino Lansky built on Grand Bahama forty years ago. My father worked in that casino, and my mother and I lived on the island with him.'

Every night after he left for work, my mother turned her face to the wall and churned tears of regret and abandonment. Every morning, equally consistently, she left for work as a bank teller in the First Caribbean International Bank. She would wake me to kiss me goodbye. I could still smell her fragrance as she left the room. One of us seemed always to be crying, and there is always a pirate in the Caribbean.

That night, back on *Adam Bonny*, I tried to go to sleep, wired as I was on various substances. Pete had prescribed me a Valium to take the edge off so I managed to drop off briefly. I dreamt of a visit to my father. I arrived on a small Caribbean island; the location was unclear. I often dream of houses that hold great promise but to which I have been denied access. And in these dreams, for one special night, I have free rein. On this particular night, my father's house contained signs of him. I could smell the cedar and mandarin of his cologne, and surveyed the neatness that characterised his appearance. More disturbingly, there were signs of his other, younger daughter by another, younger wife. I was in my half-sister's bedroom. I could see a jumble of make-up, perfume and clothes. On an occasional table she had left a small present that she had started to wrap for me. In my dream, I decided not to pry. The truth is I was not interested in what she had to give me. I wanted to find my father. I left my half-sister's room and found the door to his. I tried the handle; it was locked. In the same moment, the door to his room melted into a wall.

> *I am killed in October – and laid on church altars*
> *I am the guiser – on the bright bonfire*

I woke with a start and thought for a moment that the boat had been kicked off its moorings. I knew the boys from the estate used the dock as a short cut when doing deals. I assumed it was a runner jumping over the fence and landing badly. I had left Pete in the Brickmakers'. He 'had business to do' and had intimated he would drop by in the early hours for a session. From under the duvet I heard the creak of the unsecured hatch as it opened. Surges of adrenalin pumped through me. Someone was making their way up the galley, and it did not sound like light-fingered, wings-on-his-heels Pete.

Turnham's new boy was better than the usual piano-plunkers. In the fog and the gaslight, the noise from the Concert Hall raised a smutty haze, as a young woman opened a door on to White Lion Passage. A man wrapped in a cloak lurched over the doorstep towards her.

'For God's sake,' he insisted, 'bring me a light.'

Eliza, framed in the unlit doorway, was slight and pale. She raised her vacant eyes to his. He grabbed her arm as though to wake her.

'We've got Spring-Heeled Jack. He's here in the lane!'

It was a familiar name, doing the rounds of penny dreadfuls. She trotted into the house, not quite sure what to do. The stranger followed. Aware of his damp cloak and hot breath, she turned to hand him a candle from the mantelpiece. He snatched it from her and held it up to his face.

His eyes were red. His mouth was wet. Iron claws fell from his pockets. She shrank back into the hearth but he darted at her and tore her gown. All she could see was the voluminous cloak and butcher's hooks swirling in a nest of laces. Outside the piano plunking grew louder and voices more insistent.

'It's all done with mirrors,' the loudest said. The Lady of the Knife – whose severed head appeared to rest on the blade of a knife – had just finished her act. Members of the audience were debating her methods. Daniel's voice was the loudest. Jack stopped his clawing, fled back into the passage and was gone. Eliza fainted.

Daniel followed a strong odour of decaying flesh into the tiny court off White Lion Passage. There was an open casement in the wall. The shutter was broken and the opening low enough for him to gain access. He landed in a cellar as black as newsprint with a stream of moonlight illuminating the planking beneath his feet. His hand touched a wall dripping with mould. He stumbled against a mound of bones that collapsed to reveal a rotting carcass. He looked down to see where eyes were looking back at him.

My cat Nellie's ears were pricked. She was signalling an uninvited presence. My heart was beating loudly; my mouth was parched. She arched her back preparing to investigate. I nudged her sleeping brother aside and clambered out of the bunk. I undid the flimsy latch to my sleeping cabin. There was a muffled, creaking sound – like that of clumsy boots on rackety floorboards – coming from the galley. It was a windy night and the boat was rocking as it always did in blustery conditions. But the movements seemed to be dictated by a heavy tread. I switched on the light. For once, the electrics were working. It took a while for my eyes to adjust. The hatch was swinging open. Whoever it was was no longer there.

Days later, Daniel was lost in a thick mist, and heard a voice at his ear.

'Do you need help?'

He jumped and looked around. He could see no one, but the voice was familiar to him and somehow reassuring. 'Yes, I do.'

'What kind of help do you need?'

Daniel seized the advantage. 'An old nag to carry my load.'

There was silence.

'Just a bow-legged, scabby nag will do . . .' Daniel's words hung in the air and he faltered. Out of the mist before him came a pony, thirteen hands high, of a gleaming chestnut colour. He stabled his new helpmate. And then, just as quickly (what had he done wrong?), the pony was gone.

He sat in his room and wondered why. On the fireplace was a framed print showing lovers in a woodland glade, a bracelet of glass beads belonging to his dead wife. He married again – an Irish girl from the rebel country. They had a child, William. He learned from his mother to be industrious and followed a strict routine. Monday was washday; Tuesday all was spruce; Friday spelled a fish supper if they were lucky. Daniel had a fascination with knives. He stood outside butchers' shops to watch the spark of blades. His wife had more children. Daniel was plagued with long days and nights of forgetfulness. On coming round, he had no recollection of what had passed. He gave his fellow drinkers sidelong glances over their cups, waiting for clues.

Echoe recovered from her ordeal remarkably quickly.

'I will call you, honey,' he texted her later, 'as soon as I get one of my phones working again. Will explain when we talk or meet, hon. Don't really wanna put it on 'ere, hon. Me off ta bed now, speak soon dough, hon.' In a funny sort of way, it helps if no one is surprised or bothered.

'At de end of de day, wot's done is done! Tomorrow is a new day 'n a new start.'

An early morning carman was the first to spot her, down by Pineapple Gate on Edgware Road. The headless torso of a female was not an everyday find. Daniel trembled at the thought of what else might be found and whether he had a hand in it. Gaps in memory were plaguing him sorely. He had gone back to the cellar but could not find it. He could not look anyone in the eye. All he could remember was his first wife, and the death's head looking back at him.

That Saturday night the concert featured Biddy the Basket Woman. Daniel was not convinced. Gaudy garments and make-up concealed ulcers and rot. The new wife sewed rags on to a cotton belt that she tied around her waist. Her father, a sailor, had digs in Shadwell, by the Thames. There was a boat leaving for Valparaíso, and both men thought they were bound for a new start. They were not alone in their delusion.

So, from being a carman, the first Daniel Kingham took to water. In 1861, he reached a port in South America where naval storeships, mail steamers, missionaries and desperadoes found temporary shelter. His Irish wife remained behind to drag their children up or along in Lisson Grove. His eldest son, William Kingham, who would grow up to be a wine bottler, was a machine boy at Paddington wharf when Daniel returned to die. Every Wednesday the remains of dead paupers were thrown into holes fourteen feet deep. A clergyman gabbled through the burial service and the grave was filled with loose soil. That was the end of Daniel.

Chapter Eighteen

HERMES, GOD OF THE WASTELAND

Don't worry, Emily-Elsie. Your aunt Cecilia would have written but she ain't feeling up to it. She says I'm the only *responsible* man in the family now. So it's my duty to tell you our news. Sister Daisy made me promise to tell you that she will come to live with you one day. Then you will remember the Pleasure Dome, the dancing madder moiselles and the mud-flats . . . How you would have laughed to see us. The stage was draped in black velvet. The *fakir* (this is what he now calls himself) placed white furniture on the stage. Then the audience takes their seats, and the lights go out. In the darkness only the furniture is visible. The *fakir* (for once, Emily-Elsie, he has hit upon a goldmine) invites someone from the audience to hold his hands during the 'manifestations'. I was standing next to Daisy, laughing so hard, but we had to keep *schtoom*. You see, what happens is this: as the people watches, the table on the stage lifts up and floats in the air. The chairs follow suit. They are dancing above your very head. When the lights go up, the *fakir* invites everyone on to the stage. They marvel. They mutter. They find no clue to his mystery. Daisy is behind the stage and dressed from head to toe in black. My father the greengrocer,

god forgive him, is got up in white tie and tails. He covers
Daisy's face in a veil. It's Daisy who is moving the furniture.
But your aunt is fading. It's almost time.

'You can disappear in Southall. It's a cash economy, which
makes it easier of course. No bank accounts, no paper trail.
Yes, anyone can disappear here. It helps of course that Indians tend to have two names, Ladi or Sunni, and we're all
called Singh.'

'All right, Babbu?'

'Yeah, where was I?' Tired brown eyes ringed in purple
did a brave job of surveying me.

'What you've got to understand is that here in Southall,
everyone's up to something. Minds work like mazes: trick
upon trick until you tie yourself into knots. It becomes a
game – a game where you have to stay one step ahead. Careful you don't get lost in it.'

Carly, the girl with a sallow sad face and darting eyes, was
slinking past the window of the Brickmakers'. Before I could
ask about her, a freshie burst through the doors pushing a
wheelbarrow. He was no more than sixteen years old. He
stacked the shelves of Babbu's shops so that they never ran
dry of mobiles or mangoes. He kept the cellar stocked with
Cobras. His determination touched me in a way that I could
not fathom. In return for his hard graft, Babbu paid the freshie
below the minimum wage. He then gave an exchange rate of
71 rupees to the pound.

'Where do you come from?' I asked him. He grinned and
nodded, waiting for someone to answer.

'Jalandhar,' Babbu said, his eyes like slits enveloped in
heavy flesh. Babbu rarely spoke more than one word at a
time; his way of keeping a step ahead.

'Jalandhar,' said the voice at my side, 'is the district in Punjab where ninety-nine per cent of Southall comes from. This freshie will give the money Babbu pays him back to Babbu so that Babbu can send it back to India – "any village in Punjab, within twenty-four hours, guaranteed delivery". That's his pledge. And that's why he's a rich man, isn't it, Babbu?' Teeth glinted 14 carats in the Byzantine darkness of Spider's ruined mouth. He was in a talkative mood. Babbu waved away such childish indiscretions. He opened the trap-door for the freshie to unload his barrow. But Spider had opened the door to Babbu's secret riches.

'I've often wondered how he can keep this place going – given the lack of customers,' I said.

'It's a front.' Gabriel turned his blurred face towards me. By now, I had heard this about every shop in Southall. 'They also say he funds large shipments.' Gabriel was awake to conspiracy theories if nothing else.

'Shipments of what?' I asked.

'Drugs,' he shrugged before returning to his stupor. I had heard this about every shopkeeper in Southall.

It was always twilight in the Brickmakers'. The smut on the stained-glass windows added to the pall of hungover air. The threadbare carpet and patched banquettes just about coped with their scant load of missing-in-action Punjabi small-businessmen and broken-down drug dealers and pimps. A card game was going badly wrong in the corner of the bar, and a hand was reaching into a pocket with a threat of what might be there. Pete monitored activities from the distance of the pool table – lofty and amused, he was the permanently casual onlooker. Spider was back from a lost weekend at Jack and Jill's – the Brickmakers' best-known keepers of a crack den.

'Once I went round there, and Echoe – *their daughter* – had her head in a guy's lap. She was busy earning a tenner so she could buy a rock off her mother – who was sitting opposite her smoking crack.' Spider registered the shock he had delivered. 'On family get-togethers, they don't have a roast dinner,' he continued. 'They sit round the kitchen table, get the foil out and boot gear.'

I wondered if Spider remembered Great-uncle Danny or the twelve-year-old girl who had watched him dancing with a ceremonial sword in the garden of Woodlands Road. I wondered why, out of Danny's million-pound jackpot, there had been nothing for me. Or why it was that, when members of my family died, their houses crumbled into the ground alongside them. Their absences added up to a material sense of nothing and an acute sense of disinheritance. I had it again from my father when he went away, leaving me with photographs of himself posing against the horizon of holiday beaches. I was left with questions. Where did it all go and who was taking the photographs? As my answer I received the murmurings of old memories, and a compulsion to relive the past through writing. I also inherited the family illness. But Spider knew nothing of this. He was contemplating a forty-three-year-old white woman who spoke of being a writer while drinking in a dead-end pub in Southall. He recognised his own gambit: here was an addict looking for action in the hope that it would revive her.

'Punjabis love to travel. There's a saying we have that wherever you go in the world, you'll find potatoes and Punjabis. Unless you're the eldest son, you are expected to leave home. If you are the eldest, you stay behind to tend the land. But I think we've taken the travel bug too far. When I go back to Jalandhar, I don't even bother going to my father's village. There's no one left to visit. It's like a building site with no one on it! Most of them have gone to Canada – the number one destination. But it's cheaper to get to the UK. It costs around thirteen G. He,' pointing towards Babbu, 'has friends in the High Commission who grant six-month visas that are never renewed.'

He nodded at the freshie – brown, wiry, with a blue turban and sense of purpose. 'Punjab is the richest state in India because of guys like him, the "over-stayers". In ten years' time he will be able to go home for six weeks a year, to live like a king in a palace. That's what they work for, yearn for, put up with all this shit for, year after year after year. Back home, they're building palaces. Here in Southall, they live ten to a house, three or four to a room. None of them buys their own food. The Gurdwara provides three meals a day every day. That's the founding principle of Sikhism: an open kitchen, open to any caste. Sikhism is the liberation theology of Hinduism. All the brothers eat there.'

Nancy was smoothing her hair extensions. She had emerged from the trapdoor that led to the Brickmakers' cellar. Spider winked at me. 'The sisters, too.'

I knocked on Pete's door. Something was waiting to happen and I wanted to be there when it did. Pete's house had a 'don't bother burgling me' look of disarray and dispossession. The garden was tangled with knotweed and wire. A broken upstairs window was patched with plyboard. Through the shattered glass, I could see a long, spindly shadow curling like a question mark against the wall. The shadow righted itself, and from its arm, a crescent swung like a pendulum. A man I had never seen before answered the door. He was like a scarecrow made of patches, topped with splattered straw for hair and a beard that cascaded over the tatters and paint-stained remnants of a decayed human being.

'That was Pat the Pipe,' Pete told me later. 'He hasn't left his room in years.'

I had a restless grief I could not unravel and which burned inside me, goading me from fix to fix. Green turned to wizard-blue, and there was the Nescafé factory soaking the air in instant coffee. In this caffeine-soaked stretch of the canal, the smooth steel surface shone like a fairy castle. There were no signs of workers or inhabitants; the factory manned itself. An eerie silence presided as *Tempest* chugged along. I had lured Nancy away from Bulls Bridge and the 24-hour Tesco. We stocked up on Strawberry beers (high fruit content + 'six for the price of four' = foregone conclusion). We were drinking our way back down the canal. Nancy's designs on Soho's hostess bars had not come to fruition though she refused to say why or to discuss Plan B.

'Why aren't you married?' she asked me. I remembered what she had told me about her husband and how she did not like him, but how she had wanted to leave Ghana and her troubled family. I wondered if, like me, she had not brought her troubles with her to a siding on the Grand Union Canal under the flight path of Heathrow Airport. I could feel mine shackled to me like an overgrown child.

'I like my freedom,' I told her. Nancy misunderstood me and raised a threaded eyebrow. She had taken the promises of satellite television literally. She assumed that everyone in the Western world wanted to have sex with her.

In the Brickmakers' it was business as usual. Three women with broken limbs, splints and bandages were wrapped around Pete's progress on the pool table. They sought his protection. He legitimised their concerns. He took me by the elbow to the bar. 'You remember Scaghead Sarah,' he said, pointing to a woman with a broken leg. 'And there's Echoe.' Her elbow was fractured and she had a black eye. Coming in close behind was Carly. Her wrists were in tattered bandages and she was looking more downcast than I had ever seen her. 'There was a bit of trouble last night,' Pete pre-empted. Before I could ask for details, he parried a shot: 'You do real-ise I'm a pimp?'

'I'm here!' shouted Sheena as she made her entrance. In contrast to the others, she was resplendent. She had new hair, clothes and bracelets that she jangled in jubilation. She was high on detox drugs from her day programme. It was time for a drink if only she could find someone to stand her one.

Shock reverberated in dizzying circles around my brain. It took me ten seconds to re-adjust to my new reality.

'What percentage do you get?' I asked Pete, as though I were a potential investor in a going concern. I considered, for a moment, taking charge of marketing and press campaigns.

Closer to the dock, the old brick fields splayed out on either side, host to desultory games of football and lone, bald-headed stragglers chained to muzzled dogs. Swans sifted through so much Superwhite that the canal was bloated with bread. We docked *Tempest* by the Lamb for the sheer pleas-ure of tying off and climbing the bank into the beer garden. These were the moments when I felt I was getting warmer. Nancy shared my capacity for joy. But, like me, she was possessed by a corrosive energy that was consuming her soul. I had a connection in the Lamb – an attempted murderer recently released from HMP Wandsworth ('where the

"Fraggles" go'). His girlfriend was reputed to be handy with an axe. They were the only Punjabi customers in an old, smoky pub whose regulars had staunch Republican loyalties. These locals were the kind of people who will stop and stare when a stranger walks through the door. I got that thrill again – of having walked into a secret society in the midst of hatching a plot.

In the Lamb's beer garden, stooped over a pouch of Old Holborn, I found my winged messenger. I had gone with the flow of Lady Mary, Pete and *Bob-A-Buoy*, all of whom Southall presented in a Bollywood profusion of replenishment that sparkled, spluttered and streamed from the doorways and byways of long, drab acres of cheap housing. Spider explained that, in the Bank of Southall, Nancy was spending too much capital. She had spurned the advances of Pete despite the reasonableness of his business proposition and thought she could work on her own. Spider told me that her husband was being chased by allegations of conning Africans.

'I don't have sex with him,' Nancy reminded me, head held high. 'He's too old. No,' she said, wagging her finger. 'We watch television, and he leaves me alone.'

She went on to tell me what the pandit had told her. I had been there already. At the back of Auntie's shop where Auntie, a nice old Hindu lady, sold ready-made crack kits (an empty Martell bottle, a rubber band, sheet of foil, a pin and a straw) for £3, was a man who told fortunes.

Auntie respected her gods, and so did her customers. A miniature, ageless man with a radiant smile waited for suppliants in a cupboard behind a beaded curtain under an orange bulb. The shelves above and either side of him pulsed with dancing elephants, mouldering tangerines and many-handed goddesses.

I sat down. He made a brief remark in greeting and fell companionably into the rhythm of my concerns. He was a considerate listening presence. In the background, on an iPod, were the insistent monsoon patter and rapturous trills of a tabla and sitar. The pandit cast spells in a cramped citrus grove of a closet, an orange spot glowing from his forehead like a third eye. 'A great soul will descend on you,' he told me. 'Someone close to you will die.'

'He told me my stepmother is a bad influence. She has put a curse on my family.' Nancy splayed out her fingers to count the tragedies. 'My mother's an alcoholic. She needs a liver transplant. My aunt has Aids. She is in hospital. My brother died of a brain tumour.' Before I could catch up, she snorted at my consternation. 'I am famous in Accra. My brother was dying. The newspaper photographed me because I stopped the witch doctor frightening him. I explained to them, "He doesn't have evil spirits. He has a tumour."'

Inside the closeted heat of the shrine, the pandit handed Nancy a jug of milk and asked her to hold it before five-headed Shiva, destroyer of evil. He told her to watch the liquid ebb. She soaked up belief as a living statue looked steadily back at her. Then the pandit spoke.

'If I pay him £20, I can consult him again. He will lift the curse.' And so my friend left me behind because she did not want me to know what she was becoming.

'The pandit told Nancy that a woman was determined to destroy her.' I was now consulting Spider.

'But if she returns,' he interrupted, 'with a £20 note, he will cast a spell to confound her enemies. Yeah. That's a good one, that is. It's a cash economy in Southall. Every transaction is conducted in pounds and pence. All the businessmen keep cash and gold in their big houses on Norwood Green.

On The Broadway, they buy up to four grands' worth at a time. Because they pay in cash they don't have to pay VAT. They take the gold home and lock it up. Ask Pete.'

'I don't know what you're talking about,' Pete winked. He had the laconic grace of an expert who thinks on his feet as he scales walls. I envied him. Pete's performance was automatic and fast, freeing his mind for other things like figuring out ways and means to get the money to buy more crack and smack. He didn't even have to commit crime any more.

'I stopped burgling because I ran out of houses to burgle,' he laughed. 'Anyway, it's best to leave at the top of your game, you know, before the risks start accumulating.' He now sold security cash in hand. 'There's always snide to fence.' And he pimped women. If the worst came to the worst, there was always Auntie. She was Pete's insurance policy.

'Here in old Southall,' Spider continued, 'you sell your stolen goods to Auntie. If you haven't got any goods, Auntie will give you credit. If you haven't got any cash, you give her an empty jam jar and she'll fill it with Glen's. Basically, your needs are always met in Southall.'

I was growing tired of my addictions. The pliant course of the canal was locking me in a stone channel. As I leant towards its muddy depths, I saw myself swooning within it, unable to grip anything in its flow of weedy imagery, some of it so grotesque I scared myself. My reflection kept shocking me. My face was grey and puffy. My eyes were blank. I was thinner than bulimic vomiting had ever achieved. I could not walk in a straight line without falling over, and that was before a drink. I was frightened. It's the mundane things that get you in the end – not smoking heroin or consorting with pimps and dealers, but every fifty yards falling over. I was lurching past Emily-Elsie's grave. I was reaching my end.

But my cocaine dealers stood like silent sentinels in the Lamb. They had the menace dealers possess when they are carrying more than personal. The girlfriend wore a satchel strapped across her chest, and belted to her waist. She looked like the photograph of a putative suicide bomber that had been printed in the local newspaper. Southall had provided the press with 'Kali', a UK female insurgent. There had been a dramatic police arrest within view of the Brickmakers'. As usual, I had missed the action.

'The story of my life,' I complained when *Bob-A-Buoy* showed me the front page. But it was the photograph of Carly that caused me to stop in my tracks.

'I know this girl,' I told him. *Bob-A-Buoy*, like Nancy, shook his head.

'I'm researching the local wildlife.'

Like all the loners of Southall, but unusually for an Indian girl, Carly lived in a bedsit off Orchard Street. Pete finally told me the story. He had been to school with her. They were childhood sweethearts. ('Like Romeo and Juliet,' he sniggered.) She left him due to 'family pressure'.

The first few lines of her hotmail declaration were printed in the paper.

Raj karega Khalsa – ' "Khalsa rules", that's the Sikh separatist movement for Khalistan,' said Spider.

'I thought she was a Muslim terrorist,' I said. Spider, Pete and I were sitting round a table by the jukebox – Winehouse was refusing rehab again – and twilight was adding intrigue to our deliberations. We were comfortably drunk on news and cider – the last redoubt of the alcoholic addict. We all end up on cider. It's all we can take.

'No she wasn't a Muslim, hon.' Pete shook his head.

'Was she a Sikh?'

'No, just sick.' Pete was delighted with his pun. 'She was seeing a Chalvi.' He recomposed himself. 'Her brothers were Sher-e-Punjab. Look. She's an attention-seeker – always cutting herself and whatnot. She probably thought people would feel sorry for her if she said she was about to blow up Southall.'

A crescent-shaped anxiety carved into my memory. 'But I thought you were lovers?'

'No, honey.' Pete wanted to reassure me, anticipating a jealous rage. He foundered when it didn't happen.

Spider grinned at Pete's consternation. 'For a while, Carly got clean and found politics, didn't she, Pete?'

'Yeah. You do know it's not the Tooty Nungs and Holy Smokes any more, don't you?' Pete was growing impatient with me, and taking a swipe at Spider's past as a Sikh warrior. 'It's the Chalvis and Sher-e-Punjabs these days. And it goes all the way to Slough.'

'So what happened?' I asked them.

'Basically, one brother held her down by her feet and her mother wrapped her flag round her throat. She'd dishonoured the family, you see,' explained Spider.

'How?'

'By shagging about and whatnot,' jumped in Pete, before cueing up the pool table.

Spider picked up the story. 'Her mother said it was written in her kismet to die. But she fought her brothers off and screamed so loud the neighbours called round. She ended up at Jack and Jill's.'

'Now I told her that was a mistake.' Pete could not give the game his full attention until he had eliminated himself from inquiries. 'But she wouldn't listen. So she goes out with Echoe and ends up in the back of a Beemer Boy's car. He rapes her. I told her, "I told you not to go out with Echoe. She's always getting raped." She wouldn't listen.'

Pete sighed but felt nothing. He sucked his teeth and resumed his pursuit of the white ball. 'She got picked up by one of those Sisters R Us outfits. They found her a room and that's when she really lost the plot.'

The last time Pete came to *Adam Bonny* I found out where he was from. 'One morning, I got meself up for school. I went into the bathroom, switched on the light and there was a dead body in the bath. I couldn't see who it was at first. The walls and ceiling were like a Jackson Pollock there was that much blood splattered on them. Then I realised I was looking at my dad's girlfriend. She'd been trying to get the air out of the works. I'd seen her the night before, looking for a vein. In the end, she found one in her neck. Now it was Monday morning, and she was bloated and purple.'

Pete left me with his bedtime story, and through the porthole of my cabin I watched the hazy trails of 747s and the hints of constellations. I spied his face as he lit up on the towpath. He stood for a moment nursing his Superking cigarette. Like a spiv who deals in death he tiptoed over the rope bridge that led to *Tempest*'s moorings.

Cecilia was dying. Caster oil and ginger tea were used in the treatment of tumours. But she could not escape the force of it, pressing in on her in a room in Southend. Tired and in pain, she tried to compose herself, knowing that solitude was better than fuss. For some time now, and this was a relief, Herbert had been on the run. The curtain was down on the *fakir*, the Parisian count had been exposed. The newspaper lay open on her lap.

'A hoax, amusing, no doubt, to the perpetrator, has played upon a large number of young ladies at Southend-on-Sea. They have received letters, written in a mixture of French and English, purporting to come from a French count, possessing an estate near Paris, and staying at Southend. The writer states in each case that he has been particularly struck by the good looks of the lady, and that he desires her further acquaintance with a view to marriage. The place of meeting usually suggested is the entrance to the pier, the distinguishing mark of both parties to be a red rose.'

Below our south London flat was a courtyard. In its centre were palm trees that reminded me of my island home. When I opened my bedroom window, I imagined myself in this circle of ferns, dense with waving fronds and serrated foliage. I lifted my face to a breeze-borne scent of tropical flowers and felt the magnanimity of a universe that offered the heat of the Bahamas and suburban Streatham. Outside the sacred space of the courtyard, I lurked in dim imaginings.

'The communication trench is a shambles. Tell Daisy I didn't receive the socks and all of us boys badly need them. Trench foot is doing a better job than the Huns. The field is swept by shell-fire so that I cannot describe the exhaustion of carrying the dead and injured across it. The ground is hard as iron and coated with ice. Most of them are lying in the German wire. But I am here, Emily-Elsie, I survive to carry out the duties we all owe to one another, to keep communications open between command and the outposts in the afterglow of the sun, the echo of a voice that has finished with speaking.'

Cecilia went blind first. She was sitting in an easy chair by the gas ring. She tried not to be frightened and breathed deep. It was about time. While she waited, she remembered the house martins hawking above the pond. Mother said they were gone next morning – and the swifts that spent the summer there . . . parties of them flying round the spire. She remembered the long-eared owl that hunted in the grave-yard. A solemn face buried deep among the thorns. She opened herself up to it, and stretched in a spasm, alone in a room a few streets back from the seafront.

Chapter Nineteen

CLUB DES HASCHISCHINS

There is a bridge that stands like the mossy ruins of a Roman aqueduct over the canal. Reeds combine to create a river effect. Her scarf had caught in the prow of an abandoned boat. Swans feasted on naan bread unperturbed by her presence. She had been slashed around the face and throat until she died.

'They were trying to decapitate her.' Spider paused. He was reading the newspaper in the quiet of the Lamb. 'Her brother paid £5,000 – probably to some freshies – for an honour killing. The police are saying he sat in the pub all day so he had an alibi. He made sure his every move was on CCTV.'

Spider's anxiety forced an early removal from the huddle of grimy lace curtains, dark beams and watchful eyes. We crossed the canal, the fields and forests that have come and gone and become the avenues of Shackleton Estate. We found the President of the Gurdwara on the steps of a large temple with a golden dome. TV reporters were interviewing him as a leader of his community.

'He doesn't even live in Southall,' Spider protested. 'He lives in Gerrards Cross, where they all go when they've made their money.' His voice reverberated above the endless traffic of Orchard Street.

We were back in the Brickmakers'. Sheena was high on the drama. She rushed up to us. 'She was killed with a kirpan. Look, there's a picture here . . . "a double-edged, ceremonial sword",' she read from the newspaper.

Spider winced with grief and guilt.

'I remember your sword,' I told him. 'I remember you dancing in Woodlands Road with my great-uncle Danny.' The name triggered a knee-jerk wariness. He considered me again in the beer-stained murk, and gave in to the exhaustion of not caring who I was or what I wanted.

'That was the last thing to go,' he muttered, looking at his feet. 'I sold it to Pete for a ton.' Doubts queued to cross my mind. Posters had been plastered over Southall asking for the identity of the mystery man she had agreed to meet on the towpath. I remembered the night I had stood outside Pete's window. The image that kept returning was a revolving blade cutting through the air.

'Please put your rubbish in the chute.' Jack and Jill went up the hill. As sure as night follows day, I climbed after them. When we got there we knocked on the door and Spider shouted assurances that we were who we said we were. I was nervous of being followed by police, the dark machinations of my imagination and its attendant para- noia. With these firmly in place and with the aid of various stimulants and another friendly Valium 'to take the edge off', I embarked on my final bender. There were a couple of junkies in the living room, as well as Echoe limping but unbowed. This was the first time I had seen her dressed as a schoolgirl.

'It's so my punters can fuck me without being arrested for kiddy fiddling,' she explained. The front door was barricaded behind us so heavily that I had plenty of time to calculate how long it would take before we all burned to death or suffocated in the event of fire. The kitchen had been stripped of appliances revealing peeling paper with a brown and yellow pattern popular in the 1970s. It reminded me of a Paul Klee painting I had once seen – disembodied repetitive shapes attempting to break out of the canvas. The hobs on the gas stove had been sold for scrap. The only signs of cooking were an abandoned saucepan and a couple of cups crawling with blue moss. An empty packet of cornflour was on the sideboard. Cornflour can be put into empty crack wraps, and repackaged as 'burn', or fake drugs, to sell for a quick buck, mostly to people like me. I had 'mug' written all over me. But that was cool. Spider was looking after me. It was early evening – lighting-up time. Locals dropped by to get hooked up and do their drugs in the upstairs rooms. Sheena arrived and negotiated the rotten stairs to the bedroom with a fourteen-year-old boy with gender issues and facial piercings. My heart sank at his blatant vulnerability. River was the son of a regular client. Sheena was moonlighting as a baby-sitter. The bedroom was empty but for mattresses and buckets. The toilet was out of order. River curled up in the corner with a skunk joint. Smiler had ordered crack and brown to redistribute, as well as a bag of china-white ('strictly personal'). I matched his £50 note, and our bags arrived. Spider decided he had to sort Echoe and Sheena because they were his pals and they were doing their bit.

'I love Sheena.' River's eyes were shining. 'She's my hero,' he confided.

A few hours later there was nothing left. Sheena and Echoe had taken River hunting for more tenners to stave off the grind of withdrawal. I was frantic and my skin was crawling. I looked out of the window and made out Pete slinking into the night with Nancy. They were locked in a *danse macabre*. It wasn't murder, the police had found. It was suicide. Carly took the sword and did it for him. There was nothing I could say or do to stop Nancy. I was coming to the end of my addiction. I had to leave her to find her own.

Spider slithered down the stairwell littered with works and foil, and slid down a rubbish chute into a basement bin room. The bin men of Southall spend their nights alongside vermin underneath the twenty-one hectares of a notorious sink estate. Smiler rummaged for the sleeping bag that he had hidden the previous night between two wheelie bins. He spread it on the dank concrete floor and tried to forget the stench of refuse and the rummaging of rats in this tomb for the detritus of Southall.

Epilogue

HOW IT WORKS OUT IN THE END

Lady Mary Grey learnt English history from tracing her descent to a distant Welsh monarch, Merfyn 'Frych' ap Gwriad, or Merfyn the Freckled, King of Gwynedd and possibly Powys. From the Welsh mist of her origins, her family tree encompassed the growth of the Tudor dynasty.

For her return to Court, after lengthy imprisonment, she was dressed in a yellow kirtle and black petticoats. The yellow and black stripes combined with her dumpy shape gave the impression of a bumblebee buzzing around the Court. The code of her dress spelt 'Queen Bee'. She had not forgotten that she was heiress presumptive to Elizabeth I's throne. Elizabeth's thoughts were elsewhere, and Lady Mary Grey had been returned to favour. Even though this was a cold spring, the Plague was spreading through London. Mary became ill in April, and everyone fled the city. She stayed in her house in Aldgate because she had special protection from a 'mystic ruby'. This magical gem was the crystallised blood of a very old, very wise unicorn dating from before the time of Merfyn the Freckled. The blood was found at the base of the unicorn's horn and formed a distillation of the creature's essence. Lady Jane Grey had also owned one – it was listed among her possessions in the Tower. According to the alchemist, Albertus Magnus, mystic rubies protected against the Plague. Mary knew she was ill and she was ready.

On 17 April 1578, at the age of thirty-three, Lady Mary Grey drew up her will. She described herself as a 'widow'. She never forgot her beloved husband, even though he forgot her. It was expedient for him to do so, and she knew this. In her will, she left her luxurious new bed to her stepdaughter, Jane, and the bulk of her fortune to Jane's daughter, her godchild. She left her magical books – the books that kept her spirit alive – to Mrs Blanche Parry, a pupil of John Dee.

'As for my body,' she wrote – the least important part of her, 'I commit the same to be buried where the Queen's Majesty shall think most meet.' It was always at the Queen's disposal, after all.

On 14 May she was interred in her mother's tomb at Westminster Abbey. The Queen gave Lady Mary, her heiress presumptive, the honour she deserved, as Lady Mary had known she would.

On 14 May I was born in St Mary Abbot's Hospital in the Royal Borough of Kensington and Chelsea. Dolly made me promise I would say, should anyone ask.

Daniel found solace in the library of Paddington Radical Working Men's Club. He followed the course of his brother's career in the Law Reports of *The Times*. There were frequent dispatches. Daniel also had a younger brother who died at Flanders, a private in the Coldstream Guards. Daniel named his youngest child, a son, Coldstream. Meanwhile, the KC continued to prosper. He represented Thomas Beecham, purveyor of magical powders. Daniel came home to tell his children there was a Freemason in the family. Then Coldstream died in tragic circumstances. 'Poor little blind boy,' Emily-Elsie wailed. Coldstream went blind and died, aged seven, of blows to the head that were never explained. Silence was enforced because there was so much for Daniel to think about.

That evening, on Edgware Road, he was decorating a dairy to catch up on lost days spent in the library. It was the 5th of November, so the profusion of squibs and crackers scattered his calls and no one came. Six days later his father William died in the same ward of the workhouse.

Two years later Emily-Elsie gave birth to Danny. Of his paternity, all Dolly could verify was that there was a policemen's hostel at the end of Cato Street. 'They were tall, big-boned men,' she said. 'We used to tie a string across two lamp posts to knock their helmets off.'

When Emily-Elsie moved to Southall, Daisy followed in her caravan. She kept it parked in the old brick fields that border the canal. Occasionally, she would visit Emily-Elsie, Dolly and Danny Overton on Woodlands Road. Danny remembered Daisy charming the warts from his hand. Then, one day, like cats when they are ready, Daisy disappeared, just like the rest, no one knows where. Like Cecilia and Emily-Elsie, she could be anywhere.

On December 13 2008 I surrendered. I sold my sinking boat and crossed to dry land. I got as far as the banks of the Grand Union Canal (the Westbourne Park branch). Then I discovered that the workhouse where Dolly was born was at the end of my road. It was a TfL depot. It was here that I traced the steps of the cobbled yard where children had exercised. Like Paddington Bear in Paddington Station, I found Dolly in the Lost and Found, which spurred my desire to recover my self and my family's story. In telling it, I found out how it works. It's no great mystery. As the Sikhs say:

ਸਤਿਨਾਮ

ACKNOWLEDGEMENTS

Lilian Pizzichini is most grateful to the Society of Authors and Royal Literary Fund for their financial assistance in writing this book. She would also like to acknowledge Alexandra Pringle, Erica Jarnes, Mary Tomlinson and Alexa von Hirschberg at Bloomsbury for their support and encouragement. Special thanks go to Vivek Chaudhary and Rachel Cusk, and, most of all, enduring love and thanks to Roy Colbert.